Radio Daze

RAFE MAIR

PROMONTORY
PRESS

RADIO DAZE

Copyright © 2013 by Rafe Mair

Promontory Press
www.promontorypress.com

ISBN: 978-1-927559-27-7

First Edition: December 2013

Typeset at SpicaBookDesign in Book Antiqua

Printed in India

0 9 8 7 6 5 4 3 2 1

Dedication

To Wendy, the love of my life who has never flagged in her support of me and has from the beginning been my soul mate and to our wonderful Chocolate Labradors, Clancy and Chauncey, who loved us so much and through whom our love for each other passed.

For my reading buddy

Tony Cox

[signature]

Foreword

I had the pleasure and privilege of working alongside Rafe Mair at CKNW Radio in Vancouver during one of the most stimulating, exciting and controversial periods in Vancouver and British Columbia history. It was the 1980's and Talk Radio in Vancouver was hotter than a smelter in Kitimat. Rafe Mair was the market leader – the one you turned to – for insight, for unvarnished truth, for what the newsmakers were saying and for the stories behind the stories.

Rafe was the voice of the station, but, more importantly, he was the voice of the people – the guy who stood up for those who didn't have the money, the time, the education or the contacts to stand up for themselves. In many cases that meant the people of British Columbia – or, in the case of the Meech Lake Accord, for the people of Canada.

British Columbia was, and still is, a lightning rod for political dissent and controversy. The great thing about Rafe was that no matter who objected or got upset, he couldn't be pressured or bullied. Rafe often gives me too much credit as Station Manager for standing behind him and supporting him through difficult times. The truth is that he was easy to fight for: he got ratings, he brought advertisers and he was never afraid to make the tough call.

Someone once told me that "Managers do things right... but Leaders do the right thing". Time after time, year after year, I watched first-hand as Rafe Mair did the right thing – for the environment, for the economy, for the City of Vancouver and for the Province of British Columbia. But most of all for the people – for little guys and big guys alike – because he cared, because he could and because he was someone who worried less about making a profit and more about making a difference.

I was proud to work with Rafe – proud to call him a colleague – but more proud to call him a friend. He is an outstanding broadcaster and writer but more importantly, he is an outstanding Canadian and a generous, special human being. I know you'll enjoy his insights, thoughts and knowledge. He's one of a kind!

Ron Bremner
President
Gold Medal Consulting Group Ltd

Table of Contents

	Introduction	vii
1	My Rebirth from Politics	1
2	The CJOR Daze	15
3	The CKNW Daze	31
4	Politics from the Other Side	71
5	Issues	89
6	Life on the Media Stage	107
7	People Along the Way	121
8	People, Programs and Chauncey	157
9	End of Daze	177
	Finis	187

Introduction

This book is about a career in journalism, but as the late Denny Boyd said: Rafe Mair is not a journalist; he's a barrister pleading cases. Denny was right.

I am a lawyer by trade and, like so many of my breed, went into politics where I served as a BC Cabinet minister for 5 years. This is the story of what came after that: of the wonderful and often dizzying 25 years I spent in the media. Part of it was on TV, much of it was in writing, but the most enjoyable days of all were those spent in radio.

It's also partly the story of going gloriously broke, finding a partner who became not only the love of my life and my soul mate but the one that made my books balance after 6 years of teetering on bankruptcy.

But first, the title. When I went into radio, I was indeed in a daze. My first day on the job, I knew nothing about how one actually did this thing called "radio". I'd never done it, yet on Day 1 I was expected to get listeners by going up against the CKNW powerhouse. I was given no instructions, no dry runs, nothing. The first time I spoke into a mic was on the first day. The method was obviously "sink or swim." For example, it was a week after I started that a salesman, not the program director, who finally told me about staying "on mic" and not wandering off it.

When asked about my career in radio I reply: "I started in my 50th year, was BC Broadcaster of the Year, was twice short-listed for the coveted Michener Award, won the Michener Award, received the Bruce Hutchison Lifetime Achievement Award, am in the Canadian Broadcasters Association Hall of Fame...*during which time I was fired 3 times!*"

It's hardly a chronicle of 25 smooth and easy years but at the end of it I was able to think – what a glorious ride! I hope you enjoy it as much as I enjoyed looking back on a great quarter century and reporting on it.

As we move on, I must offer this caveat. If you read **Rafe: A Memoir** (and not enough of you did – for shame!) you will recognize an anecdote or two. I have included them for continuity in the overall tale, and rest assured they read differently from the perspective of nearly a decade later. The rest of it is all new, some fun, some not so much, and all a daze.

CHAPTER ONE

My Rebirth from Politics

In December 1980 I was British Columbia's Health Minister serving in the Cabinet of W.R. (Bill) Bennett and happy in my work. I had been in Cabinet since I was elected to the BC Legislature in December 1975, having been re-elected in May of 1979. Prior to becoming Health Minister I had held the Environment Portfolio and before that Consumer and Corporate Affairs. Before entering Provincial politics I had served one term on the Kamloops City Council.

By 1980 I was thinking about life after politics. Frankly, there wasn't any political job I craved – not even Attorney General, which would likely have been my next stop.

What about the Premier's office?

Napoleon once said that "every private soldier

carries a marshal's baton in his knapsack" and I was no exception. But there were obstacles. Premier Bennett was four months younger than I and showed no signs of leaving. I was not popular in the party nor, I judged, with my colleagues. I simply didn't want to run again and was thinking of what I could do.

Going back into law in Kamloops was not on; I had sold my practice to my partners and to move home and steal back my clients was something I couldn't do. Besides, I had re-married and to go back to Kamloops would have caused awkwardness, especially for my first wife Eve, whom I had already treated badly enough. I probably could have caught on with a larger firm in Victoria or Vancouver but I simply didn't want to do that.

I'd had one previous brush – I think that's the right word – with radio in 1972 when a client of mine, CFJC, in Kamloops, needed a host for a one-hour talk show, for a week. The regular host, the estimable Ben Meisner, was on a hunting trip. It was one hour of answering phone calls in front of a mic. There were no interviews – just phone-in. For one who had made his living answering questions from a judge on the bench it was duck soup. My stint was fun but memorable only for the fact that on the first day I ran over the 10 o'clock CBC time signal, which was, evidently, very important to many listeners.

Let me say before we get into my days in radio, two people affected my political career, which you will see morphs into the radio. Because my radio career so depended upon my political career it seems most appropriate that two people who had such an impact on my politics would appear at the beginning of the saga.

Grace McCarthy is a hero of mine. We had several interesting spats when we were colleagues, which arose because she was political and I wasn't. I was political in the sense that I had control of my constituency, as did Grace, but I was lousy at looking after "Old Socreds" and she was excellent.

When I first met Grace in 1974 she was almost single-handedly restoring the crumbled Social Credit Party. During our five years together in the first two Bill Bennett governments, she was a very powerful force. Unfortunately for her future she was seen as a "Queen Bee" by some, which undoubtedly cost her caucus support when she sought the 1991 battle for the party leadership.

I urged Grace to seek the Socred leadership but, unusually for her, she waited too long and lost to Rita Johnston by a hair. The Socreds were slaughtered in the fall election and most politicos would agree that with Grace at the helm the Socreds would, had they lost, have remained a force in the province.

When Grace did become leader and lost the by-election to Mike deJong, the party was finished, but not Grace – not by a long shot.

When a granddaughter was diagnosed with

Crohn's disease, for which there was no cure and about which little was known, Grace sprang into action as only she can do, founding the CHILD Foundation which under her immense energy (she's 86) went from nothing to $23 million in research money!

Grace is a remarkable person who never stops being so and I'm honoured to be her friend and to have been born in the same hospital – you guessed it, Grace Hospital.

I've written about **Bill Bennett** in considerable quantity elsewhere but he played a key role in my life. I have never met a man so dedicated to a task as Bill Bennett was as Leader of the Social Credit Party leading up to the 1975 election. But he had a number of obstacles:

He wasn't well known inside the party, much less outside.

He was seen by those who didn't like him as "Daddy's Boy", a lightweight. In fact he had all his father's genes and then some, although to all appearances they were as different as chalk and cheese.

Bennett Senior was outgoing and full of bonhomie, while Bill was serious unto severe with no noticeable sense of humour. In fact, in private he is a very witty man who often broke us up in cabinet. That is a side of Bill that was unknown, which is a pity.

We didn't see much of that in Cabinet for about half a year, by which time Bill was evidently content with what he had in the "boardroom" and he let himself out of the shell.

I remember with great gratitude the faith Bill Bennett placed in me. It was a great honour and a privilege to have worked with him and to get to see the good stuff of which he is made. He expected his ministers to do their job – there was no public scolding and no micro-managing. If you did your job you stayed or were promoted. If you didn't, you didn't make the cut in the next shuffle.

As a testament to Bennett's character, let me tell you a story I've never told before.

In November 1979, at a caucus retreat I made an ass of myself. I was badly jet-lagged having just come home from Japan, and I was having a hard time getting changes to the system of land appeals past caucus. I completely lost my temper and with language that belongs in the gutter I stormed out and refused all pleas from good colleagues that I return.

I went to dinner with my Constituency President that night and told him that there was a cabinet shuffle in the offing and that after my performance earlier that day, I wouldn't be in.

That night, when we got back to the room, there was a note saying "Would the member from Kamloops have breakfast at 7:00AM with the member from South Okanagan?"

This was it. I went to the Premier's room and immediately offered my resignation.

Bennett said, "Sit down and be quiet. Rafe, as

long as you are in my caucus you'll be in my cabinet, but boy, did you make an asshole of yourself yesterday and you've got me into a pickle. You've been doing the constitutional brief without a portfolio so I've created the Ministry of Inter-governmental Affairs and you were to be the minister. But I can't give it to you now because you've pissed off so many of your colleagues that you may not be able to work with them."

I started to mumble apologies and he told me to be quiet.

"I'm doing a shuffle in ten days and you have these options. You can stay in Environment: you can have the Attorney-General if Allan (Williams) doesn't want it: you can have Finance; you can take Health. Now bugger off and see if you can behave yourself."

I was stunned. I wondered if this was a dream. Or maybe the Premier was giving me the gears. I went back to the room and my then-wife Patti said, "You look weird. What happened?"

"I went to get fired and got promoted instead!"

On the day before the shuffle I was called into the Premier's office and he said, "Rafe – Allan has taken the AG but the other options are open."

I said, "Mr. Premier, I would like Health."

He came around the desk, shook my hand and said, "Congratulations, Mr. Health Minister." (Garde Gardom got Inter-Governmental Affairs.)

I realize that you only have my word to go on but I leave you with this – there were 30+ colleagues at that caucus meeting and none of them could believe that I was still in the Cabinet let alone with the biggest of all portfolios. I'm not proud of what I did at all that jet-lagged day. I was a disgrace and should have been fired. But I wasn't, because Bill Bennett gave me another chance.

I leave you with this thought - If you want to know how good a premier Bill Bennett was, just look at what we've had since!

POLITICAL BELIEFS

Because of my environmental position I campaigned actively for the NDP in the 2009 election. I have thus been criticized for flip-flopping since I was once a Socred cabinet minister.

Let me start by quoting Ralph Waldo Emerson who said, "Foolish consistency is the hobgoblin of little minds." I have no doubt that I have changed over the years. I don't think I've changed as much as many will say, but you be the judge.

When I was Minister of Consumer and Corporate Affairs I had passed, in two years, more consumer reform than done before or since. It all remains on the books. I forced the banks to obey BC consumer law, which they had refused to do so until I faced them with a lawsuit. I brought in several rule changes affecting, adversely they said, the Vancouver Stock Exchange. I made innumerable changes in both liquor licensing and distribution – amongst other things these changes effectively got rid of the hideous beer parlours. I brought in much-toughened door-to-door selling rules; I brought in the Motor Dealers Licensing Act to the horror of the five car dealers in caucus, two of whom were in cabinet with me; I brought in legislation protecting people stranded by fly-by-night charter thugs. I brought in rules and regulations that started the cottage wine industry, which has blossomed in a huge and internationally acclaimed wine industry replacing the rotgut we were producing.

For this I was despised by business and the right wing element in the party and the caucus. It must be noted, however, that I couldn't have done this without the backing of Premier Bill Bennett.

Let me tell you a little-known story and you can judge for yourself how right wing I was.

Back in W.A.C. Bennett's day there was a huge scandal called Commonwealth Trust where thousands of British Columbians lost their savings. My deputy, Tex Enemark, and I vowed that we would do everything we could to prevent another Commonwealth from happening and we kept a close look at the Securities Branch headed by the very competent Bill Irwin as Superintendent of Brokers.

One day I received a call from Bill who told me that he was having trouble with a company called Abacus Cities and wanted to see me.

"What's the problem, Bill", I asked.

He said, "Abacus Cities wants to raise money on a stock issue which I simply can't understand. There are two brothers involved and they want to see you … name of Rogers and they each sport some sort of doctorate."

I asked Bill to get them in to talk to Tex, him and me.

They duly arrived and started berating the Superintendent for not knowing his stuff, then went on and on about the virtues of this stock issue. I'd spent some time around stock markets, as had Tex. I turned to the Superintendent and asked him if he understood all this and he said he didn't. Neither did Tex.

"Dr. Rogers," I said, "I too have read the document and I don't understand it either. Until all three of us understand it, it will not be approved. Thank you for coming in."

In a few days I flew to Toronto and by an "amazing coincidence", Abacus's lawyer was my seatmate. The entire trip was spent listening to an explanation that I couldn't understand.

"Hal," I said finally, "until the Superintendent, Tex and I understand that document the stock will not be issued – period."

About three weeks later, Abacus's bank, the Bank of Montreal in Calgary, pulled their loan and Abacus crumbled like the "house of cards" it was.

There was no Commonwealth Trust on my watch. It's hard enough in politics to get credit for what you did, let alone what you didn't do!

9

Rafe Mair

At one point, the business community was so concerned about me they demanded to know from Bill Bennett when this "assault" was going to end to which he replied, why not ask Rafe yourself?

I went to a meeting chaired by Austin Taylor Jr., who was a schoolmate of mine at St George's. A very wealthy man, he was known as Firpo, once a big boxer from Argentina – Austin was a very big baby evidently. He was an enormous man!

"Firpo" gave me a mild dressing down and finally asked what I was trying to do, to which I answered, "Be a policeman in the market – as long as businesses behave they have nothing to fear."

My point of all this being that while some might think me far out on the right, that was scarcely the view big business had of me.

But no matter what my beliefs, as I said earlier by 1980 I was considering my options after politics.

ENTER JACK WEBSTER...

Jack Webster, the curmudgeonly Glaswegian, was the best radio broadcaster in the country, could spot political bullshit a mile off, and was merciless when he did. I was one of a handful of ministers Premier Bennett would let appear on Jack's show, which I did quite frequently. Not that I didn't bullshit: it was just that I enjoyed it, it showed and I could handle the heat.

It was just before Christmas, 1980. I went on Jack's show and afterwards we went to lunch in the Timber Club at the Hotel Vancouver – it was not a dry lunch. They seldom were with Jack.

After a while Jack asked me – in the strictest confidence (Jack was a man of his word) - if I was happy in politics and I told him what I just told you.

"Have you ever thought of going into radio," he asked.

"No," I answered truthfully.

It turned out that there might be an opening and he asked if he could make discreet inquiries and I agreed. After I got home to Victoria that night Jack called me and told me to call Mel Cooper, owner of CFAX, the Number 1 station in Victoria, the next morning.

"Dammit, Jack," I said, "one of the reasons I'm unhappy is that lovely though Victoria is, I don't want to live here!"

"Do as you're told, you dumb bugger," said Jack as he put the phone down very firmly indeed.

The next morning I phoned Mel, whom I knew, and he invited me to lunch where he told me that CJOR 600 in Vancouver wanted to replace the immortal Pat Burns on their morning talk show and suggested I call the owner, billionaire Jimmy Pattison. At Jimmy's invitation I flew to meet him in Vancouver the next day. Jimmy told me that he exercised no control over management (yeah, right!) but would I speak with Al Anaka and Frank Callaghan, manager and program director respectively of CJOR.

I met Al and Frank the next day and they told me they would be interested in me and what was my price?

"A hundred thousand," I answered, for a one year deal and that it was non-negotiable.

They didn't want to pay that much for an inexperienced person so we shook hands and parted. A few days later I received a call from Pattison asking how I was getting along with negotiations, as if he didn't know. Apparently Alan and Frank wished to have another meeting so I, wanting it to be on home turf, suggested the Vancouver Club.

We met and they presented a deal for $75,000 on a 3-year term with bonus clauses that could take it over $100,000 if the ratings so warranted.

I said, "I already have a $75,000 per year deal as a cabinet minister so why would I move for the same money; and it must be one year because if I'm any good I want another crack at you after a year and if I'm no good you'll find a way to dump me." They met my terms and now it remained to me to contact the premier, which I did a couple of days after Christmas.

Premier Bennett flew to Victoria straight from his Christmas holiday and came to my office. I had a bit of Scotch in my liquor cabinet, whereas in deference to his teetotalling father he didn't have a bar in his, so my office it was. He was great. He tried to talk me into staying but seeing that I was determined to "carpe diem", we talked out what and when we would say in our announcement.

(I digress to say that there were rumours flying that Bennett had a drinking problem. This was rubbish. I knew him well and traveled with him. This sort of crud unfortunately goes with the territory.)

Shortly after the New Year, I went to cabinet and the premier announced my decision, all wished me well and the press conference was then held and the job was done.

I had intended to stay on as MLA for Kamloops but as time passed it was clear that this wasn't doable. I would have conflicting interests and I would have to miss every Friday morning. From Monday to Thursday the House sat in the afternoon and evening, but on Friday it was a morning sitting to allow MLAs to get home for the weekend. So my new schedule wouldn't work since I would miss 20% of the sittings and the Opposition would have great fun trying to catch us short of a majority.

I informed Premier Bennett that I would be resigning my seat as of March 1, 1981. (The House wasn't due to open until mid-March.) Now the Premier was truly upset because we only had a 5-seat majority and my leaving would reduce it to 3 plus the Speaker. There was little danger of the government falling but a great deal of embarrassment would follow from a lost vote.

Bennett dispatched a close friend, whom I liked, Hugh Harris, to talk me out of it and I invited him to dinner and to stay with us (Hugh lived in Kelowna). We ate and partook liberally of the restoratives at our disposal until well after midnight.

The next morning there was a note from Hugh on the kitchen table thanking us for our hospitality saying he was going to catch a ferry – but that he had concluded that I was right and would so advise the Premier.

The cord had been cut and I was on my own on a great adventure.

CHAPTER TWO
The CJOR Daze

CJOR 600 was a pioneer radio station (after a name change, 600AM) and had spawned many a great broadcaster, both in music and public affairs, with Jack Webster and Pat Burns in the latter category. Their music man, Monty McFarlane, was in a class of his own. Not only did he know his music, he was funny as hell. I listened to CJOR when I was a kid and when I had my hair cut at Blakers Barber Shop in the basement of the old Grosvenor hotel I was able to watch through the CJOR studio window across the hall. And there was the inimitable and hugely popular Jack Cullen at night.

A few days before my debut Jack Webster, who worked for our rival CKNW, took me to lunch and gave me three pieces of advice in his signature Scots brogue: "Be yerself, you dumb bugger and don't try to imitate Burrrrns or me; if yer interviewing yer mither, have a piece of paper in front of you saying Mom so you don't forget her name; (both excellent pieces of advice); and from now on we're ENEMIES!"

Jack was true to his last statement, which I fully understood. I was persona non grata at BCTV as long as I was at CJOR. When I moved to CKNW (BCTV and CKNW were both owned by WIC) this changed and he hired me to be with him at several public events.

Pat Burns, a great veteran and a huge success in his heyday, learned on the 10 o'clock news on the day of my press conference that I was taking over. What a rotten thing for a station to do! I learned a valuable truth – radio stations worry about one thing only – ratings. When it comes to personnel, they are merciless unless it was in their interest to be otherwise.

As the big day approached, I kept waiting for some training to happen. It never did – not one minute. It was indeed the "sink or swim" method and when the day arrived, I was shown inside the studio for the first time. Looking back, this was probably the only way it could be done.

Just before I went on air I received a call – from Pat Burns - who growled, "Break a leg kid ... you'll be great!" Here was a class act in a business not especially known for that commodity.

The red light went on at 9:05AM and the great experiment began. My thrilling opening words went something like this: "This is a very exciting day for me ..." My first guest was federal Opposition leader Joe Clark followed by a real class act, the late Jack Nichol, president of the BC Fishermen and Allied Workers Union. His appearance on my show was not, I'm told, especially popular with the union movement but Jack was great and in the days to come all notable labour leaders were guests at one time or the other.

During this interview I faced my first real test – the power went off! The generator kicked in so that we stayed on air but the studio was as black as the inside of a goat and remained that way for ten minutes or so. I was not wearing headphones so no one could advise me as to what to do so I just carried on – which evidently was what I was supposed to do.

My last guest was a former MLA in the Socred Caucus, John Park, by then a mining man and municipal councilor.

Finally, 12:00 noon arrived and I was so exhausted I went next door to my room in the late and much lamented Grosvenor Hotel and slept like a baby for two hours.

I was in no position to assess that first broadcast – or any other, for that matter. I did get a very nice note from Terry Moore at rival station CKNW and a call from Barrie Clark, CKNW's afternoon man, inviting Patti and me to dinner in their home – Barrie was the Rentalsman when it was in my portfolio, Consumer and Corporate Affairs.

My first producer was Sallye Fotheringham, ex-wife of journalist Allan Fotheringham, and a

Rafe Mair

very good writer in her own right. It was a tough job because the "best" guests went to Gary Bannerman at CKNW where the biggest audience was. Because of the common ownership between CKNW and BCTV, Gary also had first dibs for guests who had been with Jack Webster before Gary's show had ended.

Our first ratings came out in May and we did very well indeed. Looking back, this had much to do with the "novelty" factor, something we learned with the fall ratings. In any event, CJOR wished to renew my contract then only 3 months old and I was given a substantial raise plus a car on a three-year term.

Both CJOR and I were about to learn some lessons.

Unlike TV, radio audiences tend to be loyal and stay with one station if it gives them what they want. CKNW had the best news department and sports department in Western Canada, if not the entire country. They also had great reporters like the legendary George Garrett and other audience grabbers.

It didn't dawn on me that I was up against a formidable radio station in CKNW. I just thought of myself as going head-to-head with Gary Bannerman, and may the better man win. Since I felt certain that I could beat Gary, I ignored the reality that the strength of the over-all programming of his station was the enemy.

I found out about the strength of CKNW when I

went there in 1984 and had their wind at my back. At CJOR, however, I was disheartened mostly because I listened to the applause and didn't consider that this was not representative of Vancouver listeners. We tried new things but we were farting against thunder.

Then came Jimmy Pattison's famous "Gentlemen, park your Cadillacs" memo, which started huge cutbacks. We were in a big Recession and if Jimmy was late to deal with it, when he did it was brutal.

Part of the problem was no doubt me. I was a rookie learning on the job. I wasn't getting the numbers. I didn't really know much about talk radio and it probably showed. That I did eventually learn my trade is evidenced by the years yet to come. It was just that I was too expensive to fire. I offered to take a salary cut but Jimmy refused.

Al Anaka was replaced by Ron Vandenberg ... and I was out a producer. Sallye had been fired earlier which, in spite of what Allan and perhaps she believed, had nothing to do with me. She had pissed off management and to this day I'm not sure what happened. Sallye was extremely loyal to me and I think she may just have rubbed management the wrong way. It certainly had nothing to do with the quality of her work as I saw it. One version had Sallye telling Vandenberg that he should give up his office for the big star – me!

When I asked Vandenberg what I should do without a producer he said, "I don't give a fuck as long as it doesn't cost any fucking money." When angered, Ron had a command of the English language quite like my own on (too many) occasions.

Those days I started the morning editorial at 8:30 (my start was now half an hour earlier, at my suggestion – no extra pay – in order to get the "jump" on Bannerman) a move that had some success, but not enough to write home about.

I was, however, in the midst of a controversy which I started after I interviewed Walter Stewart on his book *The Uranium Scandal*. It wasn't the first controversy I started, and most certainly not the last.

Here's what had happened. In the early 80s, the US, for security reasons (they alleged), stopped buying uranium from Canada, leaving the Atomic Energy of Canada, a federal crown corporation, stuck with a hell of a lot of uranium in stock. Jack Austin, a deputy minister and later a senator, conspired with a number of other uranium producers to fix the price of uranium. This was a cartel, something forbidden by Canadian law and international law.

Because of the fuss in part due to me and other media, the government appointed federal civil servant Robert Bertrand to investigate this mess. I knew Bertrand from my days as Consumer and Corporate Affairs minister and knew he was a good man.

In due course, Bertrand produced his paper, which was hidden from public view. Conservative MPs promised that it would be made public when they took power, which they did in 1984. The report remains buried under an unwritten political tradition which says "when in power don't make the former government look bad by releasing their buried studies or else they will do the same to you one day."

The report remains unreleased.

In general it was a tough slog, trying to put on shows that could deal with Bannerman at CKNW who, because of his numbers, got better guests than I did. He may have been better too but I've never been willing to concede that.

But there were certainly some memorable highlights. For Christmas 1983, I asked the late Bob Dawson, a freelance broadcaster, to be my Santa Claus and he agreed. I will talk more about Bob when I get to CKNW but this first time provided a laugh that Bob and I would often remember and re-tell.

A little boy came on the line and reminded Santa that he had spoken with him at the Mall last week.

"Ho! Ho! Ho!" said Santa alleging he remembered him well.

Big mistake.

Santa asked what they were all doing on Christmas Eve.

The little boy replied that they were all going to Grandma's place.

"Does Grandma make cookies or shortbread

for Christmas?" asked Santa in his most avuncular manner.

"NO Santa – Grandma's dead! Don't you remember?"

I had to take a break since we were breaking up ourselves!

One program I did regularly I called "Mair's Memories" where I would invite a well-known citizen on the show to speak a few words then challenge the audience to identify him or her. One such guest was Arthur Delamont, founder and conductor of the famous Kitsilano Boys Band. He was 90 at this time. He was duly identified and he suddenly turned on me.

"I remember you now! You were Ken Mair's snotty-nosed little kid that came to me with a cornet in hand and wanted to play like Harry James after one lesson! It was all I could do to teach you to make a noise with that damned instrument. You went home and never came back!"

The cornet went back to the pawnshop whence it originated.

Tis true!

Another guest was Ivan Ackery who had run the Orpheum Theatre for many years. After he was identified, phone call after phone call identified herself as one of his usherettes and coyly asked if he remembered her? Of course he did, then on to the next usherette.

As we closed, I apologized for not asking him if he had a family.

"I never married", said Ivan, "I never had any need to!" (As the story goes, why buy a cow when you're getting milk through the fence?)

In the fall of 1983 CJOR moved into new digs at 8th and Broadway and to celebrate we had past performers on the station as guests. Mine was Jack Short, the long-time caller at the racetrack, whose calls were later broadcast as "Jack Short's Racing Highlights" on CJOR.

I gave Jack a list of horses – Dalkeith, Goldstreworth, Avondale King, Ronrico and others and asked him to call a six-furlong race. He did and my boyhood favourite Goldstreworth won by a nose in a classic call by Jack Short, a world-class caller of races.

And then here's a story I remind myself of whenever I think I'm pretty smart.

One day I had as a guest, Lord Diplock of the British House of Lords. This was before the internet and research on people was not easy. And I had no producer, remember.

In any event I asked his Lordship about the House of Lords, its legal arm, its relationship with the House of Commons and so on.

He looked puzzled – and I *was* puzzled! I was missing something, but what?

After the program I puzzled away. Diplock, Could he be descended from Caleb Diplock whose name is tied to a very famous legal case of years ago?

That couldn't be it – and the light went on. He

23

was the Lord Diplock who had authored the famous and, in Ireland hated, rules allowing the Northern Ireland government to jail suspects without charge and without benefit of habeas corpus. One of these prisoners, Bobby Sands had starved himself to death and become a martyr.

I had screwed up – badly!

What an interview that should have been! No wonder His Lordship looked so puzzled!

THE ARRIVAL OF HARVEY GOLD

In the fall of 1983, the eloquent Vandenberg was replaced by Harvey Gold who came from Ottawa to be the new station manager.

Harvey was an extrovert and I felt confident that he would help my show by helping the entire station. My wife Patti and I had Harvey and his wife to dinner and to our usual Christmas party. I wasn't trying to suck up to Harvey but to get to know him in anticipation of working great things with him.

Alas, the new year of 1984 proved the worst of all my years save 1976 when my daughter Shawn was killed and my marriage broke up. I went through one catastrophe after another. No doubt I deserved it – most of us do play a part personally when calamities strike – but that didn't make it any easier.

My contract was due at June 30 but early in 1984 I began suggesting to Harvey that we redo it early and clear the decks for both of us. He agreed, but nothing actually happened.

Then one Saturday in early April, Denny Boyd, a well-liked columnist with the Vancouver Province, speculated that I was about to be replaced at CJOR by former NDP premier Dave Barrett. I phoned Harvey and asked him if I could come to his house, only 10 minutes from where I lived. He said, "Sure, come right over," which I did. I knew from experience that Denny had not just dreamt up this revelation and that there was probably something to it.

I came right out with it and Harvey assured me that he had no notion of replacing me, that I was "his man" and, in fact on Easter Monday, a week or so later, he wanted to "talk turkey" with me about a new contract. As a legal matter, this was to have considerable importance as, while he was under no legal obligation to negotiate with me, if he did negotiate he was under a legal obligation to do so in good faith (a concept Gold apparently had difficulty with).

Patti and I met Gold at the CJOR boardroom on that Easter Monday and he arrived with a bottle of wine, which was odd to me since a year prior I had stopped drinking.

Harvey poured the wine for Patti and himself then began reading his terms which called for me to take a $75,000 cut in pay, reduced holidays and required me to do editorials every morning (which I was doing, but on my own say-so).

As he went on I got the clear impression that I would be required to clean out the restrooms every morning. Every question I asked, large or small, was met with "request denied" – just those two words.

At noon, Harvey said, "there it is, take it or leave it".

I was scheduled to have a week off in one week's time, doing a trip to Washington and Columbus, Ohio at the expense of the US State Department to learn how the national budget was put together by Congress and the President and then the relationship of the State government and the Federal government. I suggested to Harvey that he let me have that time to get my thoughts together. He replied, "request denied" and declared that negotiations were ended.

Patti and I were in a state of shock. We expected that we would take a pay cut but assumed that we would have some say in it. The rest was so belligerent that we simply couldn't believe it. For the balance of the day we talked about it and for the first time I learned what bad financial shape we were in and that, amongst many other things, we owed three years' income tax!

I have no desire to rake this revelation over the coals except to say I was an idiot to have given the entire handling of the family finances over to Patti and for not exercising any supervision. The fact was we were not only broke: we were a net $250,000 in debt. This was the recession and our house was worth less than the mortgage, we were in debt to the bank and the Tax department and all our credit cards were maxed out.

It was clear to me that I had to get things back on track with Gold so the following morning at 6:30, my usual arrival time, I left a very conciliatory note for Gold on his desk, asking for another chance to negotiate. Surely, less than 24 hours later, Gold wouldn't refuse this request.

He did and it became clear he had agreed to hire Dave Barrett with whom he had been negotiating all along.

At the end of my show Harvey called me in and said that negotiations were over. CJOR would not be renewing my contract. I was still in shock, but assured Gold that I would do my best to do good shows for the rest of my contract. He said that if I disclosed any of this to anyone he would stop paying me immediately. He only owed me until the end of June.

I was in big trouble, for how was I to look for work unless I could tell why I was looking?

It came to a head when a couple of days later I had a local journalist, Rick Ouston, on my show and I asked him in a station break whether I could ask him something in complete confidence?

He agreed and when I asked him if there were any media spots I might try for, he immediately said, "I'm sorry but this is a big story and I'm going to use it. You can expect the TV cameras when you get off air." After I pleaded with him he agreed to send the cameras to my house at 1:00 PM. I should have known better to trust the bastard but I was desperate.

At the end of the show I tried to see Gold but he wouldn't see me so I went to the program manager, Frank Callaghan, and told him what had happened and suggested that we issue a joint statement simply stating that, regrettably, we were parting company, no hard feelings etc., etc.

Frank told me he would talk to Gold about it and that I should phone him from home and he would give me Gold's position. I duly phoned Gold, who told me that he would not take this "high road" but would issue a statement that I had refused a generous contract, blah, blah, blah. He immediately couriered me a letter saying that my services would end on June 30.

In desperation, I phoned Jimmy Pattison but he simply said it was a business decision made by Harvey and that was that.

I was done, like dinner. No job, no assets and flat broke.

The really hard part was the firing – it was a very public affair in all the media. I tried to do the right thing but Gold was hell-bent on disparaging me publicly, which he certainly did very effectively.

I spoke to my lawyer, Mike Hutchison in Victoria, who advised me that Gold/Pattison had not dealt with me in good faith and that I should sue – which I did. A few months later I received a phone call from Jimmy saying that he was upset by what had happened and would I talk to one of his men, without lawyers?

I phoned lawyer Mike, a friend indeed, who told me to "fly at 'er" so I phoned Jimmy's man Bill Sleeman and agreed to meet him the next day at the North Shore Winter Club.

We met and Bill asked what I wanted. I said I should be paid what I would have earned in those months since I was fired. Bill agreed and a few days later I got a cheque for nearly $50,000, all of which went to the Tax Department.

It had been a steep learning curve, I'd come into radio with no experience and most of what I thought I knew was wrong. I went through the phase of psychics, astrologers, numerologists, authors who couldn't write and minor politicians on the make. I did a lot of "free-for-all", that is to say open line without a guest, just head to head with listeners, something that I loved. I learned that lots of phone calls did not mean lots of listeners. I listened to the regulars whom I got to know by name and who helped me out, especially in the later months where I had no guests because I had no producer.

I also gained respect of many of my colleagues, which made it easier being fired for at least no one in the media kicked me when I was down.

In summary, I learned my trade at CJOR, which enabled me, in due course, to kick their pants off. I made some good friends and, with the obvious exception of Harvey Gold, left no enemies. At the end of the day, Pattison treated me fairly.

There is an amusing postscript.

About 18 months after I was fired I had a serious operation and in the Recovery Room, neither the staff nor Patti could wake me fully. I had been 6 hours under anesthetic. Evidently Patti, thinking it might get my attention, told me that Harvey Gold had been fired (as he indeed had been) to which I evidently replied, "There is a God!" – and went back to sleep!

CHAPTER THREE
The CKNW Daze

BUST AND OUT OF WORK

By October 1984, I was desperate. My home was in foreclosure and, as I mentioned, worth considerably less than the mortgage. I owed huge amounts although I had quieted down the Tax Department with the Pattison money. I was barely making enough to feed my family while trying to pay off debts, and I wasn't even entitled to welfare. I remember the irony of me, not a sou in my pocket, looking out from our swimming pool across the Vancouver Harbour to BC Place and muttering, "that's where those down on their luck wind up ... why am I any different?"

I supported Patti and my kids, Kim and Steve, by doing a variety of things.

Richard Hughes, then part owner of Sunshine Cabs in North Vancouver, gave me some

consulting fees. I did some consulting for Bur-
ston-Marsteller Public Relations (I saw first-hand
how lies were gussied up into "facts"). I was
making a bit of money consulting for a couple
of Vancouver Stock Exchange Companies (from
which I much later made about $50,000) and other
odds and sods. It was enough to eat on but didn't
substantially reduce my obligations. I must also
thank from the bottom of my heart the legal work
Mike Hutchison in Victoria did for me pro bono
… it made a huge difference.

ON WRITING

During this time I leaned heavily on my ability as
a writer, and I'd like to take a moment to describe
my writing career, which was, as you will see, an
integral part of my broadcasting career from the
outset.

Not long ago, I came across my old Prince of
Wales High School graduation annual and I was
astonished to find I wrote seven articles and also
did the music page – Rattling Records with Rafe –
in the school paper The Three Feathers (referring
to the crest of the Prince of Wales). They are pretty turgid prose but there I was, a writer

The wonderful humourist of the 20s and 30s,
Robert Benchley, once said: *"It took me 15 years to
discover that I had no talent for writing, but I couldn't
give it up because by that time I was too famous to
quit!"*

I'm far from being in Benchley's league but I do find that a healthy part of my income over the years has been from writing – in fact most of my income if you count editorials I did on radio for nearly 25 years.

I didn't do much writing after High School until 1975 when, as MLA for Kamloops, I wrote columns once a month for the late Kamloops Sentinel and the Kamloops News. With the exception of one done on a visit to Hiroshima, which makes me weep when I think about it today, these columns were typical politician's bullshit - but I did have a byline.

My first professional column was for the late and much lamented Financial Post in 1981 (it's now a section of the National Post – quite a different thing). I wrote for them off and on until 2001 when Conrad Black bought it and gracelessly informed me of my leave-taking by simply sending my latest column back with a note saying they didn't need it anymore. I was mad as hell at this because my friend Diane Francis was my editor in latter days and she was fun to write for. Moreover, the pay was good, as was the publicity.

In the late 80s while writing for Diane, Globe and Mail Editorial Page Editor Sarah Murdoch offered me a column for a tiny bit more than I was getting at the FP. When I told Diane she became quite upset and called the Globe "those fellatio performers"(at least that was the gist of what she called them) and then said, "What will they pay you, $50 more a column? I'll raise yours $75!" – in fact Sarah only offered me $25 but Diane didn't leave me time to answer her question, so I "reluctantly" accepted the raise. I said, "I'm glad someone loves me." The next morning a huge bouquet of flowers arrived at the radio station with a card saying, "we love you".

It was the high water mark of my writing career, and I do get quite a charge of being able to say that I turned down a column with "Canada's National Newspaper". I did so because it was to be "a view from the West" and I had to tell her that I knew next to nothing about what people in the Prairie Provinces thought and it would be wrong to pretend that I did.

I wrote for the Vancouver Courier twice and left on the best of terms. I also wrote for the Georgia Straight, and ditto my leaving for one of my stints at the Courier. With other employers the leave taking was less happy. The "Now" papers fired me, for which I was truly sorry since I was syndicated and making good money. I was fired by a family magazine whose name I've forgotten - actually they went belly up so perhaps that wasn't a firing after all. I wrote for the David Black chain of community papers for a few years and they definitely fired me on purely political grounds – they were hard "right" and I wasn't. Fish farms, which I oppose, were my death knell in Black papers on the coast. I was also fired by the North Shore Outlook.

I did, however, have the pleasure of actually

firing the Vancouver Province for whom I had done a column for a couple of years.

In 2005 I began writing for The Tyee (wwwthetyee.ca) under the editorship of the estimable David Beers who, like me, had taken his lumps from the mainstream media. At this writing, eight years later, our relationship is excellent. Sometimes I've had to change the syntax and be brought up short on potential defamation but I've had a complete free hand with the content.

During my radio career, I always had at least one writing job, some times more than one and more often than not I had a radio and/or TV gig. This meant that on every tagline was my name and for whom I was broadcasting. This was wonderful advertising and articles frequently became part of my radio shows through the open line. Every one of my editorials was written beforehand, not off the top of the head as many did. I did these for every program for 25 years and that took a hell of a lot of writing! In addition I did editorials on TV – many of them with BCTV, CTV, CKVU, City TV, Joy TV, City TV (Victoria) and others. All these, of course, drew attention to my radio show – priceless promotion of my show.

I can say with certainty that I wouldn't have been as successful as I was as a broadcaster without the writing.

But in 1984 neither my writing career nor my broadcasting career were paying the bills, and Patti and I were facing homelessness and poverty.

Then some luck broke my way.

Grace McCarthy and her husband Ray threw a bit of a cocktail party, where I met John Plul, the superb publicist for CKNW who asked me what I was up to. I told him that I wanted to broadcast but that no one wanted me and that I was thinking of going back to law. This was on a Saturday night and John asked me to go out to the station on Monday morning at 9:00. I, of course, agreed.

When I arrived I was ushered into the office of the Station Manager, Ted Smith, and was astonished to see all the brass there.

After preliminaries, Ted got straight to it. "We're thinking of starting a new talk show to run from midnight until 2AM to be called Nightline BC, on the WIN Network around the province – the pay would be $90,000, with you providing your own producer."

I was back! And with the top station in Western Canada! Patti would produce – she had helped me during the last days at CJOR - and since the program was mostly open line producing wouldn't be that tough. While I still had my work cut out for me, I could start reducing my debts.

Ted says I asked to use his en suite bathroom and emerged to say a resounding "Yes!"

I wasn't quite there, however, since CKNW had not made a final decision and the starting date was a month away. It was, to say the least, a stressful month.

By the time I reached CKNW in November 1984 I had learned a hell of a lot about broadcasting, including about how the real issue was not just who was doing the broadcasting but also how strong the overall station was in its advertising, community activities, public relations and corporate policy. Let me quickly add, though, that the broadcaster was the knight in shining armour and if he played his role well, the station did well too. The opposite is also quite true, as witness the fact that Bill Good has been an utter failure in replacing me.

CKNW was what's called a "heritage station", meaning that listening to it was a rite of passage. It was sort of "until 30 you wouldn't go near CKNW, after 30 that's all you listened to". Before getting to my arrival, here's what the great – as indeed he was – reporter George Garrett saw in what he dubbed the 'NW story.

They say it takes a great hockey team to win the Stanley Cup.

In the competitive world of commercial radio it takes a team to build a station. Such is the case with CKNW, soon to be 70 years old!

CKNW was the dream of one guy, a salesman named Bill Rea. With studios above a hotel in New Westminster, CKNW went on the air in 1944 with a crazy mixture of country and western music (as it was then called), folksy interviews and, probably most important, plenty of news and sports.

Rea hired a local kid named Jim Cox, who became a very good play-by-play broadcaster of New Westminster

Salmon Bellies lacrosse games and New Westminster Royals hockey games. Cox also became the News Director, doing an on-air shift and running the newsroom. NW became the first station to put a reporter on a beat. It was Mark Raines, who would later become a Talk Show host on CJOR and a Member of Parliament.

There were no news cruisers, no pagers, and of course no cell phones. They didn't exist. Mark was on his own in his '53 Ford and a pocketful of dimes for payphones. In the late 50's NW added a night shift news cruiser and the first sponsored news vehicle in the market. It was the Sunbeam Bread Radio News Cruiser ... complete with a facsimile of a loaf of bread, the "top dog" logo and CKNW in big letters. The first guy to work the night beat was Bill Fox, better known as "Barometer Bill" for his on-air weather forecasts. Bill was followed by George Garrett, later described as the "Kid from Moose Jaw." Garrett worked the night beat for many years, and later the day beat and got to know police officers, lawyers, elected officials at all levels from park and school boards, to city and municipal councils to provincial and federal governments. As well he knew street people - pimps, prostitutes, drug addicts and criminals. Among his friends on the downtown east side was a lady named Margaret who sold newspapers at Carrall & Hastings. When her cat had kittens she put them in a box and took them to what was then called Magistrate's Court at the police station at Main & Cordova, where she knew George would be covering the courts. She wanted him to see her kittens!

George's contacts helped him broadcast stories that

sometimes beat the opposition. One rival reporter said he wanted Garrett's casio (electronic contact list) when he died.

Garrett is still living at age 78! He retired in 1999 with one last scoop. On that very day Gordon Wilson bolted the Liberal party and joined the NDP, George broke the story.

The best of the best decisions CKNW management ever made was to move announcer Warren Barker to the newsroom. He succeeded Jim Cox as News Direc-tor and assembled an incredible team of editors and reporters, including the first women to work in radio newsrooms. Warren set the standard by his own hard work and integrity. People who worked for him not only respected him, they adored him. His shift technically started at 5 AM but staff noted that each year his shift would begin earlier and earlier, even 2 or 3 AM. His copy was crisp and clean ... never a word out of place. It was so well done that Hal Davis would merely have to scan the copy before reading the 8 AM News "live."

Competition among radio stations for news cover-age became intense. Other stations began hiring beat reporters and put more emphasis on news. CKNW re-sponded by introducing news every half hour and in-serting bulletins from the newsroom...complete with the sound of teletypes for breaking news. (They also had a prize for anyone who sent in a good news story – RM). *The news beat for a day shift reporter working alone included the cop shop, Magistrate's Court on Vancouver's Main Street, County, Supreme and Appeal Courts in the old courthouse on Georgia and City Hall at 12th & Cambie. As well, the reporter had to cover breaking news including bank hold-ups, homicides, fires, labour strikes and anything to do with politics. It was a learning experience for all reporters who had to have a little knowledge about a lot of things but not a lot of knowledge of any one thing. There just wasn't time to be a specialist in any particular subject.*

The evolution of news coverage came with the introduction of open line shows, sometimes called hot line shows. Pat Burns was making a big impression with his hotline show on CJOR. Jack Webster was lured to CKNW to counter Burns and the battle was on. Burns left town (some say he was forced out) and Webster switched to CJOR for more money. It was panic time at NW. The station developed "The Investigators" which included Gary Bannerman, hired from the Vancouver Province, the late Ed Murphy, Terry Spence and a guy named Jacques Khouri. Only Bannerman survived and went on to become a very successful Talk Show host. Sad to say Gary died too young a few years ago.

While Bannerman helped NW there was still the problem of Webster on rival CJOR. It was a stroke of genius: then-Manager Ted Smith cut a deal to have BCTV hire Webster, with NW picking up part of his salary. It worked because both CKNW & BCTV were owned by the same company. It was a win-win situation. Webster was very successful on TV and CJOR was destroyed by the loss of Webster.

The Talk Show format was a godsend for NW News. Reporters were able to expand their news stories, complete with tape clips to give listeners a better under-

standing of what was happening. While coverage on newscasts was restricted to 40 second stories, reporters could be on the air for several minutes on Talk Shows giving the kind of coverage that was previously found in the print media. Radio news became so successful that newspaper newsrooms had the radio on and would not miss an NW newscast. While radio and TV had been pirating newspaper coverage for years (and still do) the shoe was now on the other foot in many cases. Sun reporter Kim Bolan said publicly late last year that when she began as a rookie, her job was to listen to NW News. She said, "I would be told "Garrett's got this... can you match it?"

Their actual programming was hard to beat, starting with Frosty Forst in the morning drive, followed by Gary Bannerman then Barrie Clark; then the afternoon drive with Rick Honey followed by Dave "Big Daddy" McCormack, then Jack Kyle and the inimitable Jack Cullen rounding out the day. And there was "Big Al" Davidson on sports. It was an all-star team. But most of all, it was the news room that made 'NW unbeatable.

At 8:00AM the big newscast for the entire Lower Mainland was read by Hal Davis, who always closed with "have a good day, d'ya hear?" It was the highest rating time, by far, in the market. In radio what you leave as an audience when you're through is critical. I would re-learn that lesson later on when I was fired by CKNW in 2003.

The 8:00 News was followed by Al (Big Al) Davidson with the sports as he saw it, which was always emotion provoking, usually anger, and not necessarily having much to do about sports . But, as one friend once said to me, "I hate the bugger's guts but I haven't missed a word he's said in years!"

At 8:30, it was Earl "The Pearl" Bradford, sort of a modern day Hedda Hopper who had a large following. One cannot overlook Bill Hughes and "Roving Mike" where he would interview visitors at the bus stop. ("From? Oh, Tashkent? My wife and I were there a couple of years ago." Less than gripping stuff but very popular.)

Then the Clifford Olson horror arrived in the summer of 1981. Kids went missing, parents panicked – it was a horrible time to have teenage kids and I had two. George Garrett had a long and solid relationship with the various police forces and scooped everyone on the Olson case almost on an hourly basis, which didn't hurt CKNW's ratings and we at CJOR got slaughtered in the summer and fall ratings.

But I have left the best to the last: John Plul, promoter extraordinaire, who first invited me to come to the station for a job. John was a one off. He wasn't like most PR men - he didn't tinker with the truth. What he did was keep CKNW, its logo and its product before the public at all times and in many different and unusual ways.

An excellent example came in 1982 when the Vancouver Canucks were in a key playoff series with the Chicago Blackhawks where in one game

the Canuck bench, protesting what they perceived to be a bad call by an official, waved tow-
els. The next game was two days away and when
the Coliseum opened every fan had a white towel
with CKNW prominently emblazoned on it, courtesy of the fertile mind and never ending energy
of John Plul.

Warren Barker, perhaps the best newsman
in the country, gave editorial comment after the
6:00PM news. On the weekends, Jon McComb
and Leigh Mackay kept the audience, and in Terry Moore the station had a superb back-up broadcaster. When I was at CKNW he did my programs
and on vacation he did what he was supposed to
do – keep my audience for me. Terry was in a class
by himself when it came to doing remotes, such
as a car lot, where, because the car lot guy was
scared stiff, Terry would, in effect, interview himself.

And then Rafe Mair was added to this team.
Here's how George Garrett generously told of my
early days at CKNW:

*NW offered Mair the Midnight to 2 AM spot, ob-
viously buying some insurance if Barrie Clarke decided
to leave his Noon to 3 PM spot. It was no secret that
Clarke and (Garry) Bannerman detested each other, so
much so that the station had to build a wall between
their desks in the Holiday Inn Studios. Eventually
Clarke did leave to write a book and Rafe moved up.*

*Mair skillfully blended his knowledge and love of
politics with his newfound ability to communicate on*

the radio. Always a fierce debater and one who chafed at authority in any sphere Mair soon found he was having the time of his life. He knew the political game just as well or better than the people who played it. His interviews were often tough, usually informative and seldom dull. It was fun giving them hell whether it was Bill Vander Zalm, Mike Harcourt or any federal politician who would face him. Some would not.

Most political observers in BC would rate the 1986 Socred Convention at Whistler as the best ever. The stakes were high. Who would succeed the retiring Bill Bennett, a premier who had had Mair in his Cabinet and a man Mair respected.

Would it be Grace McCarthy, who had saved the party from oblivion or would it be one of the "Smith Brothers" - Brian Smith, the Attorney General or Bud Smith, the political operative from Kamloops? Or might it be Bill Vander Zalm, the sometime maverick Cabinet Minister from Surrey.

Not everyone was aware that Vander Zalm had some wealthy supporters, among them a developer from Richmond and Peter Toigo, who somehow managed to buy Nat Bailey's famous White Spot chain and was very interested in getting licenses for new pubs. Toigo spent big at the convention, hosting delegates in a tent. He was not registered as a convention delegate and could not legally get on the convention floor. However, he must have had an urgent need to speak to Vander Zalm or his key people. He "borrowed" a name tag from none other than Edgar Kaiser, scion of the famous family involved in the coal business in south eastern BC.

Excitement at the convention was palpable. Vander Zalm led after the first ballot with Grace McCarthy second. Broadcasting "live" Mair got a signal to throw to floor reporter Garrett, who told him and his listeners that Bud Smith was going to Vander Zalm. Mair could not believe it. "Ridiculous," said Mair, "that wouldn't happen in a thousand years."

But yes, it had happened and Vander Zalm won, launching a zany period in BC's political life.

Mair predicted that Vander Zalm would destroy the Social Credit party within two years. But at least it was a fascinating ride for all those involved in covering the provincial political scene. Although abortion was a federal issue Vander Zalm let his personal beliefs prevail to the embarrassment of his own Attorney General, Brian Smith.

*Smith later resigned over what he perceived as interference by the premier in his role as the attorney general, a position that should not be subject to political interference {*Grace McCarthy also resigned alleging Vander Zalm interference- RM}. *Vander Zalm wanted to know if he was under investigation, as he surely was. The issue was the sale of his theme park, Fantasy Gardens, to an Asian investor. The optics of that deal would have made a good movie script. Faye Leung, a lady known for her outlandish hats, claimed Vander Zalm owed her money as commission for the sale. Her allegations made great copy. $20,000 cash in a brown paper bag had changed hands at the Bayshore Inn in the wee hours of the morning and Leung said she was cut out. Her famous quote was, "He (Vander*

Zalm) got 20,000 bucks…and I got nothing." The scandal ultimately led to Vander Zalm's resignation in one of the more bitter resignation speeches ever given by a British Columbia politician.

All of these stories of course, were fodder for newscasts and talk shows alike.

It was during this period and in the years following that Mair often had reporter Garrett on his show talking about the issues. It developed into a weekly dialogue and they did not always agree. News Director Gord Macdonald, Garrett's boss, never did like his reporters expressing their opinion but Garrett got away with it. It got to the point where Mair began calling Garrett "The Intrepid Reporter." It was a name that stuck and it sent the high school dropout reporter to the dictionary to find that "intrepid" meant 'fearless, dauntless, courageous, very brave'. Garrett thought it was a bit of a stretch but he never demurred.

Back to Rafe. 1984 was a terrible year and it still took 6 more years to pay off my debts, made no easier by sending the kids to College and trying to get Patti to understand plain arithmetic and to pay the taxman - promptly. I don't blame Patti alone. I should have stepped in much earlier and even after I did I still left matters in her hands which led to a couple more blood-curdling monetary moments such as, when property prices came back considerably, getting a $65,000 mortgage to pay off the latest income arrears Patti had managed to run up after two years when I was back working; then borrowing $50,000 from her mother which, I'm delighted to say, was not only paid back but Dot made a tidy profit.

But 1984 – the year from Hell – was over and I was with the "Top Dog". They were the news station of record. I couldn't believe my good fortune!

A bad year turned into quite a ride in the years to come.

THE MIDNIGHT SHOW (NIGHTLINE BC) 1984-85

I was over the moon at going with CKNW – I immediately got a CKNW bumper sticker - and proud as punch; it was a feeling that was unaltered for all the years NW were owned by Frank Griffiths.

There were some dodgy moments for certain, but that comes with the territory when you are doing an aggressive political talk show on the leading edge of politics in British Columbia.

The station managers when I was there, Ted Smith, Ron Bremner and Rod Gunn, all had some moments when anyone would have been tempted to let me twist in the wind. But they didn't ever do that. They never interfered and always supported me no matter how heated the advertiser might be.

Just before my first show, Gary Bannerman, now sadly gone at much too young an age, had me on as a guest on his morning show. From 1981 to 1984 he had been whipping my ass regularly in the ratings.

"Hi Rafe," he started, "what have you been doing the last few years?"

We both had a good laugh and some banter.

I always liked Gary and while I sure would have loved to have beaten him when I was at CJOR, Gary was experienced and, if a bit ponderous, very intelligent and well informed. As it is to so many broadcasters, John Barleycorn was his big enemy.

On my 50th birthday, after evaluating the situation, I concluded that most of my friends – and I - were drinking too much and, seeing and feeling the pressures of broadcasting, I quit drinking and stayed on the wagon for 12 years. As much as anything, I wanted to find out if it would be a problem. Happily it wasn't.

Since then I will drink my beer but no hard stuff, happy in the thought that if I hadn't adjourned the exercise when I did I might have died at 59 as my Dad did. Now at 81 I can relax a bit.

In those days the CKNW talk shows studios were located in the Holiday Inn Harbourside, now the Mandarin. We were on the top floor and the view of the North Shore Mountains was breathtaking even at night. While I am terrified of heights, because we were in the midst of a broad terrace I was OK. (There is nothing rational nor funny about phobias, by the way. When CKNW moved us to the 21st floor of the Toronto-Dominion Building they had to build a special spot for me to broadcast from and the blinds were always pulled. My own office was not at the window as had been planned but an inside one. I took special "safe" routes to and fro.)

On my first show the Manager, Ted Smith, came on to introduce me and told the audience that I would be a fine broadcaster and he only hoped that I stayed away from cruises (Gary's favourite pastime) and baseball. (My first guest was the late Senator Ray Perrault who was busy trying to get a major league baseball team for Vancouver!)

The midnight show was a lot of fun – it was a different audience. We had cops and hookers, graveyard shifts and insomniacs and folks who were just "night" people. Because it went around the province we had miners and cowboys around the fire.

Back on air, it wasn't long before I tested the patience of management.

One guest was the famous gourmet chef, James Barber, on to talk about fine restaurants and like stuff. I opened the lines and a caller, for some reason, mentioned "McDonald's" and my witty response was, "I had one of their burgers about eight years ago and every time, to this day, that I burp I can taste the damned thing."

I mean what the hell, McDonald's wouldn't be listening at that hour and, besides, they had a good sense of humour didn't they?

Yes they did and no they didn't.

The next morning Ted Smith invited me to lunch – not a good sign – where he told me that not only was McDonald's pissed off but they had written to Mr. Griffiths demanding that I be fired!

"Rafe," said Ted, "we stand behind our broadcasters but if you feel the urge to smooth things over, here's their manager, Ron Marcoux's, phone number."

I said, "Ted, if I have to apologize every time I poke at a client I won't last long… Fuck 'im!"

"Fair enough," said Ted.

I went home and phoned my lawyer, Mike Hutchison in Victoria, and told him what had happened. He informed me that the McDonald's letter to Mr. Griffiths amounted to incitement to breach of contract and that they were in more legal trouble than I was.

I thought about this and said to myself, "Rafe, you dumb bastard, what you said was stupid so why not admit it and phone Marcoux?"

I did and when he came to the phone I heard myself say, "Mr. Marcoux, this is Rafe Mair and I'm not apologizing!

"Nor am I!" Marcoux replied.

There was a pause then we both started to laugh.

I then said, "Mr. Marcoux, the McDonald's story is a hell of an interesting one – why not come on my show and tell my audience about it?"

"Good idea", said Ron – now no longer Mr. – Marcoux, "and the day we do it I'll take you to lunch, and no, not at McDonald's!"

Shortly thereafter I phoned Ted to tell him peace had been declared and he replied, "I know – Marcoux just phoned."

Thus ended my first, but certainly not the last, of my brushes with management. It also told me that CKNW did believe in free speech and would back up its broadcasters.

One night, having no guests, I decided to play my own version of Trivia, which was all the rage then, called Sexual Trivia, where listeners were encouraged to tell a funny story about sex in their lives. I said at the start that while this was the middle of the night and we could be a bit risqué, let's still keep it within reasonable limits.

I must tell you at this time that we had a "kill" button. The broadcast was 6 seconds after the words were spoken so the broadcaster could delete bad stuff. I never mastered it and in moments of panic couldn't remember if I waited 6 seconds and hit the button or whether I hit the button and waited six seconds or what the hell to do.

The sexual trivia went swimmingly. One lad described how after his girlfriend's parents had gone to a show they went up to the master bedroom and after a frolic or two, blew up some condoms and, starkers, batted them around like they were balloons. At this delicious moment, the parents came home having got the wrong night for their show!

Towards the end, one guy used the term "blow job" (this was before Bill Clinton) so I went for the "kill" button with all the uncertainty I mentioned above.

The following morning Doug Rutherford, the

Program Manager, called me and congratulated me on a great show but asked, "what was it you bleeped out?"

"Why do you ask?"

Because what came out was, "bleep, bleep, bleep BLOW JOB!"

One of my guests, at midnight mind you, was Rick Hansen who was starting his "Man in Motion" trip around the world in a wheel chair. No one else was interested in interviewing him.

When Rick returned from his incredible odyssey, I was on the afternoon show, and when asked by everyone for an interview Rick said, "When I was about to start, the only one who cared was Rafe Mair and his is the first interview I'll do."

A class act.

THE EVENING SHOW AND
THE AFTERNOON SHOW – 1985-88

For some reason the "brass" at CKNW decided to get rid of the Dave "Big Daddy" McCormack music show that followed Rick Honey's afternoon drive show and do "talk" instead and I was asked to move to 6:00-9:00PM slot. I was delighted to take it. Not only were the hours better, it was a promotion - but at the same salary.

(Until the early 90s the station vastly underpaid me. I believe they knew how badly off I was financially and took advantage of that. My evidence comes later in this narrative when I finally hired an agent and learned how much I was actually worth.)

My move corresponded with the re-location of the talk shows to the BC Place building on the Expo '86 site.

The evening show was a difficult show for Patti to produce. Guests were hard to come by at that hour – even more so than at midnight - so much of it was dealing as best we could with what we had and take a lot of phone calls. We did get the occasional celebrity like actor Michael York but it was tough sledding.

One of the perks of radio was "contra" which meant you could use a client's product without paying for it as the client knocked it off CKNW's bill. "Contra" was often used to sweeten contract negotiations – you had to pay full price and the value went into your income thus was taxable. At the time I was "moonlighting" with a company doing some business in London so with a few days off I used some "contra" with British Airways to go to London.

I had scarcely arrived when I received a call from Patti telling me that Barrie Clark had quit the afternoon talk show and that I might want to contact Doug Rutherford, the Program Manager, who had promised me that if either of the two other talk shows became available I would have first dibs. Indeed that's what I'd been led to believe was the reason for hiring me in the first place.

I called Doug who confirmed Barrie's leaving but was very coy about who would replace him and said that I should check in with him when I got back.

I did so and Doug told me that they had 76 applications for the job including some pretty big names. I was pissed off to say the least.

About two weeks later, just before I was going on air, Doug phoned me and asked if I would come to the main office in New Westminster the following morning to be interviewed for the afternoon show. I told him to go to hell – I wasn't like some bride being ogled on the dock by prospective husbands: I was a known quantity and wasn't going to be "auditioned" off as if I were a teenaged newsreader from Swift Current. They could go to hell.

It sounds weird but I knew that if I begged for the show I would be like an employee and I wasn't but an independent contractor. The tax implications of this distinction were enormous.

Doug phoned virtually every station break and my answer was the same.

He called when I got off the show and pleaded with me to come and that it would be a meeting to offer me the job. That's what I wanted to hear and on that basis I agreed to be there.

I arrived at CKNW the following morning and all the "brass" were there including manager Ron Bremner who simply asked, "Doug, I understand that you recommend Rafe for the afternoon show?" Doug replied that he did so Brem said,

"Rafe, Doug thinks you are the man for the afternoon show – will you accept it?"

I replied, "Yes." There were handshakes all around and the entire affair was a done deal in 60 seconds, max.

I was told that the money would be reviewed when my contract ran out at the end of the year and like a damned fool I agreed. I got a very small raise but not as promised but as we shall see, what goes around comes around.

The afternoon show was successful in that it got good ratings and was in an exciting year.

One of the best things about moving was that Patti would get help, which she did from Donna Freeman, a very capable producer who in fact did most of the work while Patti spent most of her time to establishing contacts.

THE MORNING SHOW, 1988-2003

When Gary Bannerman left in June of 1988 and the station hired Jack Webster for the summer, I had no idea what they intended to do so I just kept my counsel and waited. In due course they asked me to take the show and I accepted. No more money but again, dear friends, patience – it's coming. Apart from a modest pay hike during the afternoon show I wasn't making much more than I did with the Midnight Show.

At the beginning of September 1988 I took over the Morning Talk Show and couldn't help observing that I had come a hell of a long way in a very short time. Who would have thought that less than four years after I had been gloriously and publicly sacked by CJOR, and in disastrous financial shape, I would be top of the heap on the #1 station, CKNW? Certainly not I.

CKNW IN THE GOOD OLD DAYS

I got to the #1 spot with huge numbers as never seen before.

I'm the first to admit that it was hardly just Rafe's doing – I relied on the whole broadcasting team and those who backed them up. I also knew that the CKNW of those days wasn't going to put just anyone on the air and that in a real sense the success of one required the success of others. CKNW and I both succeeded and I was proud of that. I mean that not as a gracious compliment but as a statement of reality.

I also knew two other things – if I didn't get the numbers I was toast and that if I ever showed weakness (as opposed to contrition when I was wrong) I would lose the respect of my audience. In that latter regard I had to treat my own station as I would any other big player in our community. I didn't enjoy being crossways with my station and criticizing them on air, and when I did, I was sometimes scared.

I had seen with my own eyes proof of what I just said from actions by Al Davidson, Frosty

Frost, Gary Bannerman, Jon McComb and others. And Jack Webster and Pat Burns before them. You got no brownie points by not standing your ground. At no time did I say things on air about CKNW for fun or to show-off. While standing my ground, it was gut wrenching.

A very good example of this happened in 1988, a few months after taking over the morning show. Gary Bannerman had a drinking problem and went over the top and got fired. You can imagine how I felt, just a few months later, when Doug Rutherford called me into a meeting to tell me that CKNW was hiring Gary back as the fill-in host when regular hosts were away.

I had no fear of Gary – I considered myself a better broadcaster and if I weren't, I deserved to be fired and receive the very handsome golden handshake Fin had negotiated. My concern was that I was converting Gary's audience and I was extremely happy to have Terry Moore as my sit in. Terry was an excellent broadcaster and kept my show going for me.

Doug then let it out – the reason they wanted Gary back was they had learned that he, along with former CJOR manager, Ron Vandenberg, proposed to buy rival station CFUN and Gary would be my opposite number. It was an old CKNW trick – if you were scared, pay 'em off. CKNW had bought off the opposition before with Jack Webster back in the early 70s as an example.

That evening I heard Doug on the BCTV six o'clock News saying that they were hiring Gary because he was such a fine broadcaster and that, he assured one and all, it had nothing to do with a rumoured involvement of Gary in the ownership of CFUN. This meant that the next morning, as I got ready to go on air, I had a major consideration – what would I do when a listener raised this issue, as was bound to happen. A good part of my reluctance was that I didn't want to encourage a public quarrel about Gary, his abilities or habits.

I knew I couldn't lie nor support a lie, so I opted to deal with it right off the top, before the editorial.

I said, "You may have seen our Program Manager on TV last night saying that CKNW was hiring Gary Bannerman back and that it was simply because of his superior abilities and had nothing to do with the story that he was going into competition with them. That simply was not true. That Gary was rumoured to be part of a new talk station up against us was indeed the real reason. I have no more to say about this either now or on open line segments or anywhere else. The issue as far as I'm concerned is closed."

I heard nothing from the station either then or any other time.

I must say this about my last Station Manager, Rod Gunn. He was not a talk show sort of man, but more music and he was in charge during some hard times with me. When I asked people to cancel Vancouver Sun subscriptions, and during the lawsuit with Siddon, he was unwavering in his support. The move was indeed really none of my business and I don't really know why I got involved. He was around at the time of the Siddon case and the Simpson case and gave me full support.

The fact is that Rod – like Ted Smith and Ron Bremner - supported me when lesser souls wouldn't have.

MOSCOW AND MCDONALD'S

In 1990 the station thought it would be good idea to send the show to Moscow. It was after the Berlin Wall had come down but the USSR was still intact, with Gorbachev still in power promising perestroika and glasnost. It was an interesting time indeed.

The station hired a Russian agency to put the trip together, to look after accommodations and specifically to ensure that the guests spoke English since we were broadcasting to our home. Shirley Stocker, one of the ablest producers in the business, would produce the show and I would host it.

We arrived in Moscow to find ourselves with hotel rooms you literally could not swing a cat in and several miles away from the studios. We soon learned that every guest on the list only spoke Russian but a translator would be provided - for a fee, of course. Shirley had two days to put the shows together.

She did it.

The local manager of British Airways helped immensely by putting us in contact with McDonald's which happened to be opening the first McDonald's in Moscow near Gorki Park. This was being done by the Canadian parent company and they all but adopted us. In a day they had us moved into the National Hotel, the best (still a dump by our standards), which at least had rooms you could swing a cat in, but best of all, the hotel was right across from Red Square and the Kremlin.

Proving why she was the best in the business, Shirley put together four shows, with interesting guests including the deputy mayor of Moscow. Joe Adamov, a veteran Soviet broadcaster, whom we knew and who had appeared on my show, was a big help.

It happened that the Canadian Brass was playing at the opening of McDonald's and they agreed to open our shows with the Russian National Anthem and O Canada. They were super.

The technical arrangements were through Gesteleradio, the national radio and TV company, run by a very dour man named Gennady who treated us very well.

Getting to the studio was by cab, which you could only get with a package of Marlboro cigarettes. Drivers weren't the slightest interested in money - what the hell. They got paid whether they drove or not, so why drive? The cigarettes did the trick but just why it was Marlboro's is unclear.

The shows themselves were pretty mundane affairs with good but not terribly exciting guests unless you were interested in how the Soviet system worked - or did not work. The most exciting time was when Gennady was four minutes late getting us on air leaving Terry Moore at the CKNW end tap-dancing, at which he is in a class of its own!

It was a very interesting time to be in Moscow.

The experience of Moscow with money at this time was head shaking. When we arrived at the airport we had no rubles for it was against the law. There were no porters and a buggy cost 5 rubles although a porter could be had by either $5 or British pounds, both worth much more than 5 rubles.

We had much to learn. The legal exchange was 1 ruble, 1 dollar. At the hotel, it was 18 rubles to the dollar. In the tunnel between where our hotel was situated and Red Square, it was 32 rubles to the dollar.

The check-in at the hotel had a dozen people where a large hotel here might have two, three at the most. They had no computers and they used an abacus for working out money matters. (So did the huge GUM department store at Red Square.) On each floor there were two ladies to give you your room key then take it back when you were going out. They were reputed to be where you used the Black Market.

At the GUM store there were three line-ups, one to select the item, one to pay, and one to collect your purchase after you had paid. (Oddly, this is the exact system used by BC Liquor stores when I worked in them in the 50s as an underage university student!)

The strangest part, to me at any rate, came at the duty free store at the airport.

One is not supposed to take any rubles out of the USSR and I had about 300 of them left. I spied a neat camera for 250 rubles in the Duty Free shop so I told the clerk I would buy it.

That would be for $250 US I was informed.

"But the US dollar and the ruble are officially at par and the ruble is your means of exchange! And, this is a Russian Duty Free!"

No dice, I got on the plane with 300 hot rubles and no camera.

Prices in general were skewed. $300 a month was a professional's salary but the rent probably $20, while a car, after a 5-year wait at least, would be too expensive for the vast majority of Russians. This monetary distortion ran through the system. The best book on this is Hedrick Smith's **The New Russians.**

I mentioned McDonalds.

The line-up to get in on the first day was three blocks long. Shirley and I ate our cheeseburgers at the official opening the previous night and I can assure you that they are the same as at home and I'll say no more on that. McDonalds was just super to us. In addition to arranging the hotel, they took us on their tours and to the Bolshoi for an opera.

I loved Moscow and the people and I want to go back and will.

THE CKNW NEWSROOM

The CKNW of the Frank Griffiths/ WIC days may well be remembered for Talk Shows and for controversial hosts like Jack Webster and me (I says modestly) but the foundation of the station and all it accomplished was the newsroom.

The man who made the CKNW newsroom was the inimitable Warren Barker – in fact under him the Newsroom would be in the running for the best in Canada.

Barker had John McKitrick as his sidekick and he would have made a fine news director and I simply don't know why he didn't become such. My sense of it was he simply didn't want the job. And Barker was a hell of an act to follow.

Barker's ethics and standards were impeccable and he tolerated no sloppiness. The reporters he turned out were all first class in that vein.

George Garrett was in a class of his own, but others were top rate and I risk offending my operation of an aging memory by singling out Yvonne Eamor and Jon McComb who, if there was a brain in the present day outfit, would have the morning talk show instead of Bill Good (who gives the word "dull" an entirely new meaning).

Any of us on-air hosts could read the ratings and we knew that when we went on air, no matter what hour, we followed a newscast that left us with great numbers. As mentioned, the 8:00AM newscast was the most listened to quarter-hour of the day.

I was scarcely the first to use reporters on a talk show but I was the first to do it regularly. They were instructed by Barker to give news, not opinions, but I daresay I did drag a little bit of opinion out of them from time to time!

In the Vander Zalm years George Garrett was a virtual regular on the show and in those days there was no need for opinions because the mere reporting of Vander Zalm and his government created plenty ready-made opinions.

The news was, of course, followed by the sports, which for most of my time meant Sports Director Al "Big Al" Davidson, who in fact was shortish and stoutish.

I remember when I was first hosting the afternoon show Davidson did an editorial just before my show telling the world what a jerk Rafe Mair was – he sneered out the words "lawyer" and "politician" and in the latter sneer he compared me very unfavourably with Grace McCarthy – which was fair enough.

During the break following this "sports" cast

the program director Doug Rutherford phoned me and asked me not to respond.

"Bugger that," I replied, "Al's forgotten who has last word. Or, more likely, he doesn't think I have the guts to respond. Either way, he's wrong."

I said my piece and was never bothered by him again. Indeed at the racetrack a few weeks later I saw Big Al, and a bit later there was a bottle of wine on my table courtesy of Al Davidson.

Davidson had two motorboats on which he used to take fishing parties and from which he would report the fishing news to 'NW. One day, one of the boats was in dry dock and burned unto destruction followed, in an amazing coincidence, by his other boat just moments later. The insurance company refused to pay on the basis that Davidson had started the fires himself.

Al admitted that he had started the engines of each of them, on shore, but he didn't know that these actions might start fires! He won the lawsuit and was reimbursed for what were by then known as Charcoal I and Charcoal II.

Davidson smoked Galois cigarettes, which smell like hell. He used a dish with water in it as an ashtray and when a lady in the newsroom asked him to stop, he threw the ashtray contents into her face.

The end came when he threatened to kill his colleague Neil Macrae, who took it seriously. He was fired and immediately started with CJOR. At his first opportunity he said that leaving 'NW was like leaving Belsen (a notorious death camp under the Nazis).

Davidson sued CKNW for wrongful dismissal and before the trial Doug Rutherford asked me to look at the transcripts of the Examinations for Discovery and give an off the cuff opinion. I said simply that Al's case was this: the station had allowed and even encouraged outrageous conduct by him in the past, so why complain now? And I said that the court would likely be sympathetic to his position. As it was.

When Davidson won and 'NW appealed they asked me what I thought would happen and I said, "You'll lose." And they did.

You may think I'm being boastful here but it's true and I think any member of 'NW, lawyer or not, who had seen and heard Davidson's shenanigans in the past would have said to the 'NW brass, "It's a bit late - you brought this on yourselves."

Radio stations always lose defamation cases (the big exception being Simpson v. WIC, CKNW and Mair which, as mentioned, they won by a 9-0 decision in the Supreme Court of Canada.)

The reason they lose is that courts, without saying so, evidently believe that hosts will say anything in order to get ratings. I can't speak for colleagues but in my case I don't believe this is so. I believe that free speech can only be our basic right as long as we test it. Certainly I did some tough stuff but whenever I felt uncomfortable with an editorial I "lawyered" it with the best in the business, Dan Burnett, and accepted his suggested changes unhesitatingly. At no time in my 25 years did we do something "just for ratings".

When I was wrong, I apologized. Moreover, I had a personal rule I strictly adhered to – never hit the little guy. Concentrate on the big kids, the ones that have all the power.

As I mentioned, to retain the essential liberty of free speech, the limits had to be tested from time to time. I had been in the public eye as a politician and had a lot of things said about me that I thought were untrue, yet I've never taken a libel action. Most of my political colleagues had the same policy that was fortified when NDP MLA Dave Stupich, of Nanaimogate fame, sued then Premier Bill Bennett over a trivial matter and lost, looking terrible in the bargain.

This began, I know, as an assessment of the CKNW newsroom and part of their remarkable record under Warren Barker was not only the accuracy and fullness of their reporting, but their courage as well.

That sort of newsroom – and my sort of broadcasting – is, alas, no longer fashionable.

THE MONEY IMPROVES – DRAMATICALLY!

From the beginning of my time with CKNW I had always felt that I was being deliberately underpaid because the company knew that I was fighting bankruptcy. The money I was making was certainly much more than most Canadians earn but it's a question that finds its parallel in sports and movies – with such large revenues, what share should go to the performer? (And remember that Parkinson's Law, which states that expenses rise to meet income, applies to everyone including me! Except with me, it should read "surpass income".)

During my time at CKNW I always was top in the ratings. To give some idea of what I mean, CKNW now has 9% of the available listeners. If I'd ever had a 9% share I would have slunk away, tail between my legs. My share varied between 17% and just over 20%. But this did not reflect in my earnings.

Every Wednesday afternoon, a good friend of mine, Fin Anthony, and I used to fly fish the Sunshine Coast for Sea Run Cutthroat. It was a great tonic.

Fin had been in the advertising business for years and knew the media market very well indeed. One day Fin said, "I get the feeling that you're not happy with CKNW. If you don't want to talk about it, that's fine I'm just asking as a friend." I told him what I was being paid and a look of horror came over his face.

"If you want me to be your agent for the usual fee, I'll double that amount plus get a $50,000 signing bonus."

"But," I said, "I'm not very far along in my present three year contract. ... How can you be so sure?"

Fin asked if I was compelled to do my editorial off the top, to which I replied in the negative. In fact I told him that one of the reasons I felt short-changed was that my editorial got such high ratings.

Fin said, "That's the bargaining chip we have. If you were to stop doing the editorial it would cost management a bundle not just in the editorial time but in that your overall numbers would drop. Leave it with me but you have to stay to hell out of the negotiations or I'm gone."

Two weeks later, trying without success to conceal a smile, Fin said, "I've failed you – I've doubled your fee but could only get you a $40,000 signing bonus! It's a three year contract and they have to pay you a year if they want to fire you."

Needless to say I was overwhelmed, especially when CKNW held a cocktail party in a large prestigious hotel to celebrate, a party attended by the mayor of Vancouver and Premier Mike Harcourt.

When I needed a friend, Fin was there.

This also enabled me to finally pay off the burden I'd been carrying since 1984.

CHAPTER FOUR

Politics from the Other Side

BILL VANDER ZALM AND ME

When Bill Vander Zalm was Premier he certainly gave us lots of interviews and stories. Vander Zalm was the former mayor of Surrey who, like me, won a seat in the Legislature in December 1975. We'd served in cabinet together until I left in early 1981.

It would be hard to find anyone who didn't like Bill. Good looking, exuberant, and charming, he was easily the most popular minister in the Social Credit party. He was the embodiment of right wing politicians, having promised in the 1975 election to give "welfare bums" a shovel and, indeed, he auctioned off signed shovels, which were great sellers at Socred fundraisers.

But he had a fundamental flaw – not only was he incapable of forming a consensus, he instinctively opposed them with a "my way or the highway" approach.

Bill became leader of the Social Credit Party in July of 1986 after Bill Bennett retired. The leadership convention was at Whistler and while more than a dozen sought the prize it quickly came down to Grace McCarthy; insider and my former campaign chairman, Bud Smith; attorney-general Brian Smith (no relation) and Vander Zalm.

I helped cover the proceedings for CKNW. After the first ballot, it got down to the "four" and during the break between the first and second ballot, our ace reporter George Garrett reported that Bud Smith was crossing to Vander Zalm. I scoffed and as George indicated, I expressed my disbelief and as I did, I looked at the convention floor and there was Bud shaking hands with Bill! Shortly thereafter I was told that when my show ended Bud wanted to see me. When we met, Bud said that his people told him that he didn't have enough second ballot strength and that joining Vander Zalm now would ensure a cabinet seat. (In the event, Vander Zalm did not put him into Cabinet until late in his term which Bill much later told me was the "dumbest thing he ever did". That admission covers a lot of ground.)

At the end of Ballot 2 only Vander Zalm and Brian Smith were still standing and the following day the "Zalm" won handily.

On the day before the last vote Bill Good, who was covering the dust-up for the CBC, to which I was accredited as a commentator, asked me, on air, what would happen if Vander Zalm won?

I replied, "Within two years he will destroy the Social Credit Party."

I was spot on. Why was I able to make this prediction?

Only one of the caucus and no cabinet minister supported Bill and the only backbencher to do so was Jack Davis, whom Bennett had fired from cabinet in 1976 for getting his office to get him first class air tickets which he turned in for Economy tickets, pocketing the difference. Not only was Vander Zalm not supported by former colleagues, most of them either ran against him or actively supported other candidates. In short, almost the entire backbench and cabinet had a death wish for the new premier. I must add that, contrary to appearances at leadership contests, the losers and those who support them think that the winner was actually a serious mistake and that they or their chosen candidate would do a better job. At times of tension, which leadership contests provide plenty of, the "I told you so" crowd add to the leader's grief rather than being of loyal assistance.

Notwithstanding that, Bill Vander Zalm won over Brian Smith handily. He was helped by the fact that the previous afternoon BCTV and the Vancouver Sun published polls showing that of all the candidates only Vander Zalm could beat the NDP in the next election. I said then and say now that this was improper meddling. They weren't publishing breaking news but news they had themselves contrived, the only purpose of which was to interfere with the democratic process happening at Whistler. It foretold days to come when the media became, as it is now, like a house paper for the far right wing Fraser Institute and the governments it supported.

The Vander Zalm years, 1986-89, ended when he resigned because Conflicts Commissioner Ted Hughes found him in a conflict of interest, a concept that many politicians just can't grasp.

The Vander Zalm years were tumultuous to say the least. In the last year before he resigned, four of his backbenchers had left caucus to sit as independents. (As the wag said, the difference between a caucus and a cactus is that with a cactus the pricks are all on the outside!) There were the resignations from cabinet by Grace McCarthy and Brian Smith. This brought Bud Smith in as attorney-general but, by the time I was on the morning show, he had to resign when, as AG, he stated, in a phone call that was taped by an outsider, some nasty criticisms of a lawyer acting in a case against the Crown. He was also overheard making sweet talk to a female reporter, which included making a date where he would bring the wine.

As an old friend it was pretty hard for me to call for his resignation as I did while he was listening. It was especially hard since we were sort of "kissing colleagues" at my old law firm. His wife, Daphne, my last articled student, had stayed in the firm until she became a Supreme Court Judge thence to the Court of Appeal. Bud was, for a time, an associate in the firm.

(Perhaps this is an appropriate time to lay to rest the notion that after I was in government I received benefits from my old firm. That is plainly untrue. I had left my firm on December 22, 1975, and had no connection thereafter although they continued to use my name – as I write this it's called Mair, Jensen, Blair – which they are entitled to do. Blair has for some time been a Judge on the Supreme Court.)

During 1986-88 there was scarcely a day went by that George Garrett wasn't on my show with the latest madness from the trivial - Vander Zalm getting a neighbourhood pub licence for a close political ally and fundraiser's girlfriend - to him entertaining a shady Filipino billionaire named Tan Yu, to whom Vander Zalm was trying to sell his theme park, Fantasy Gardens, at Government House.

But the Zalm was not without his fans and they became very active in trying to shut me up.

There was a lady from Salmo who called almost every phone-in session telling us, amongst many things, how charming the premier had been to her.

The station manager, Ron Bremner, who fielded as many as he could, was swamped with phone calls from what we called the "Zalmoids". But "Brem" was made of stern stuff.

He then sent a memo to all bulletin boards in the station announcing in terms that were at least equal to positions taken by John Wilkes, Thomas Paine and Thomas Jefferson, saying that what CKNW had for sale is "free speech".

Brem was the right person for the job.

My criticism of Vander Zalm had embarrassing moments.

At a CKNW/BCTV Christmas dinner I was seated with Bill's son Wim, who did a very popular Garden Show on 'NW. To my horror there was a moment when he and I were alone at the table.

Wim said, in a soft voice, "Rafe, you were unfair to my Mom and Dad this morning."

I replied, "I think you're right, Wim, and as Bill's son you have every right to criticize me."

I had been unfair, although accurate in the sense that my facts were correct and this outlined a problem – but I had overreacted. When frustration sets in you lose your objectivity which I had clearly done.

Before leaving this subject I must say that Bill Vander Zalm not only didn't whine about me but at a roast for me in 2000, he was a roaster and sang his version of "On Top Of Old Smoky" which was a riot! He understood the role of the media and, though he didn't like it, knew that it came with the territory. We have remained on good terms.

HORSE TRACKS AND HORSE HOOEY

I had long been a horseracing fan and since moving from Victoria to Vancouver was a constant attender at Exhibition Park. I know a bit about the subject, having been a fan since a child.

Exhibition Park is 5 furlongs, (5/8 of a mile). This makes the turns much sharper than the traditional one miler, of which we once had two - Lansdowne and Brighouse in Richmond. Owners of good horses are reluctant to subject them to the sharp turns at Exhibition Park.

In 1986-87 a new one mile track was bruited about with the owners of horses cheering the issue along. Then Attorney-General, Brian Smith, had called for a "Santa Anita North", clearly ignorant of the fact that the real Santa Anita in California was having serious fiscal problems.

The co-owner of Exhibition Park, Jack Diamond, showed no inclination to get involved. The wealthy horse owners – the late Herb Doman and Russell Bennett to name two – were all for a new course but held tightly to their wallets. Owners all saw themselves in the Walter Mitty mode, in air-conditioned boxes sipping mint juleps and expecting someone else to raise the bucks and take the risks.

I did several editorials on this making these points.

Pretty soon the hype began for a new one-miler either at the old Colony Farm near Coquitlam or at Burns Bog. No one even had an option on either of these pieces of land nor any approval from zoning authorities. To make a track pay would require an average of 25,000 patrons a day, six days a week, and there was no public transit that would take people from Vancouver to either of these proposed sites. It was, in fact, all a pipe dream that none of the dreamers wanted to get personally involved in.

In fairly short order I was getting hassled in The Terrace at Exhibition Park, where we had seats, to the point my wife and I simply stopped going.

Incidentally, the reason that Brighouse and Lansdowne ultimately folded was for lack of decent transit from Vancouver to Richmond. Sadly, shortly after the decision was made to do all racing out of Exhibition Park, the Oak Street Bridge was opened and people would have been able to get to Lansdowne fairly easily.

Both Lansdowne and Brighouse are now shopping centres.

CONSTITUTIONAL CRISES – MEECH AND CHARLOTTETOWN

When the Constitution (The 1867 British North America Act) was brought home from London in 1982, Quebec refused to sign on, claiming they had been robbed, especially of their perceived right to veto any and all constitutional changes. The Quebec Court of Appeal unanimously rejected their argument as did the Supreme Court of Canada, unanimously, with all 9 judges sitting.

In the 1984 general election, Brian Mulroney, a bilingual from Quebec, was the Conservative leader and badly needed seats in Quebec so he promised constitutional reform acceptable to Quebec which would with typical Mulroney hype, "make Canada whole again".

It was political bullshit. Quebec separatists had lost a referendum on sovereignty in 1980 and there was no appetite for more constitutional dust-ups. But for Mulroney some "luck of the Irish" happened.

In 1986, in Edmonton, following the request of Mulroney, Premier Vander Zalm and his provincial counterparts, in a meeting without their officials present, agreed to postpone their constitutional demands until Quebec had hers satisfied.

It was breathtaking stupidity! Nine premiers utterly lost their minds. The obvious consequence was simple – Quebec would have a veto over all constitutional changes before any other constitutional issues were dealt with. Issues such as Senate reform, so important to Alberta and especially British Columbia, yet opposed by Quebec.

By giving Quebec a veto there would never be any changes to the constitution without her consent! This was utter madness with the only sane person in the room being the Quebec premier, the late Robert Bourassa.

I spoke many times to BC's Deputy Minister for Constitutional Affairs and my former colleague – and good friend - Melvin Smith, QC, who was utterly appalled at what the premiers had done behind closed doors at a wine-sprinkled luncheon without officials present. Mel, a man whose experience in these matters went back to being constitutional advisor to W.A.C. Bennett, simply could not believe it.

No doubt Mulroney could not believe his good fortune and he convened a First Ministers' conference at the Prime Ministerial retreat at Meech Lake, in July 1987. This was the meeting that spawned the Meech Lake Accord, which would create Quebec as a "distinct society" and gave her that cherished veto. The deal had to be ratified by all provinces and the Federal Government by June 1990.

By that date two provinces, Manitoba and Newfoundland and Labrador had not signed on. (Actually Newfoundland and Labrador had passed the resolution when Brian Peckford was premier but when Liberal Clyde Wells took over, he promised a new vote.)

In the 18 months or so prior to the deadline, Clyde Wells was damned-near a fixture on my show. Provincial Liberal leader Gordon Wilson was one of the few politicians in any Canadian government opposed to Meech Lake and I was the only media person opposed. Gordon was, needless to say, a regular guest and often brought Wells, giving me many interviews in person and by phone. Clyde Wells was so popular that his principal aide, Deborah Coyne (later the mother of Pierre Trudeau's daughter and recently a candidate for leadership of the Liberal Party) claimed that he had received thousands of letters, faxes and flowers from British Columbians supporting him.

With just days to go, the Manitoba premier, Howard Pawley, called the vote on Meech but, technically, because of short notice, he needed unanimous leave of the legislature and a backbencher, Elijah Harper, a native, refused to give it. Meech Lake was dead. As a consequence, Premier Wells did not call for a vote for the simple reason that since Manitoba had nixed the deal, there was no need to. Why foment anger and rancour unnecessarily?

Mulroney was enraged. Instead of taking it out on the Manitoba Premier Howard Pawley or Elijah Harper (bad politics to badmouth an Indian) he dumped all over Clyde Wells.

(A footnote re Manitoba: I don't believe for a moment that it was an oversight by Premier Pawley to not call for the vote earlier. Premiers are not built that way. It was a deliberate way to take the heat off Manitoba itself.)

What now?

Mulroney went back to the drawing board and the Charlottetown Accord was born. This deal, Mulroney bellowed, in a speech in French to Quebec, was Meech Lake PLUS! PLUS! PLUS!

The principal difference between Meech and Charlottetown was the latter added a new Senate, which would have been an even worse joke than the present one. Constitutional expert and Liberal MP Edward McWhinney, who was a professor on that subject with Simon Fraser University for years, called it a "damp squib" which, in my view, flattered it.

Mulroney pulled out all the stops and called in all his markers to get support for Charlottetown and as a result had Business, Labour and the artsy-fartsy segment all behind him. He also had, initially at least, the politicians, federal and provincial – of all parties except Gordon Wilson - in his camp. What he did not have was Pierre Trudeau. The former Liberal PM was retired, but still extremely influential, and outspokenly against Mulroney.

There was this major difference of process between Meech and Charlottetown – the former called for support of provincial legislatures and Ottawa while the latter was to be a referendum. Technically, there were two referenda, one for Quebec and one for the rest of the country. BC had passed legislation calling for a mandatory referendum for any proposed constitutional reform. Because of Meech, the government knew that British Columbians would skin them alive if the Legislature took the responsibility that the people considered theirs. Every province had to approve and it's now forgotten that Nova Scotia was the first to dissent.

So far as I'm aware, I was the only regular journalist to oppose Charlottetown apart from Gordon Gibson and former BC Deputy Minister for Constitutional Affairs, Melvin Smith, QC, who were occasional columnists and who both gave me substantial support.

The campaign was not without its amusing moments.

Early on in the campaign, CBC's The Journal convened a panel in which I was included. The others were all in the Calgary studio but I was in the Vancouver Studios staring into a glass eye. The subject was whether or not BC would support Charlottetown.

I listened as a pollster told us that BC would indeed vote "yes" because it enthusiastically endorsed Meech. (I muttered to myself "don't say bullshit!") Two others also stated in essence that once Mr. Mulroney went to BC and when Labour, Business and the intelligentsia came here, we would see, understand, and support their wisdom.

Again I murmured to myself "DON'T SAY BULLSHIT!"

Bill Cameron, the host, then asked me what I thought and I said "RUBBISH! There isn't a chance in the world that BC will support it … you must all be smoking something illegal!"

The CRTC had apparently warned CKNW that during the campaign my show had to be even-handed and that everything I said would count for the "NO" side. I had, in fact, done all interviews with YES people, including the federal

minister Joe Clark, their spokesman. He was pa-
thetic, with red blotches on his face and shaking
hands, showing clear signs of the pressure he was
under. At one point I made what to me was an obvious point that with Quebec holding a veto over
all constitutional change, the only route left to BC
was to threaten to secede.

"That's wrong! Wrong! Wrong!" he yelled.

I yelled back, "It's right! Right! Right!"

Somehow that somewhat-less-than-inspiring
exchange played out on the airwaves across the
country.

Mulroney aide Derek Burney (whom I had met
some years before in Seoul when I was a BC minister and he the Ambassador to South Korea) informed us that if Charlottetown didn't pass, the
US would refuse to trade with us, the very next
day, and the country would fall apart!

New Brunswick premier Frank McKenna told
us how the day before he had spoken to a group
of veterans in Victoria, and told them that if Charlottetown failed, their fallen comrades would
have died in vain. I told him that he could not
have said a stupider thing and that he and the
YES campaigners just didn't understand British
Columbians, but they soon would.

On the Monday a week prior to the vote, I advised the audience that Prime Minister Mulroney
would be on for the full show on Friday – his office had confirmed this - and who better could
make the pitch for Charlottetown?

I reminded the audience on Tuesday that the PM would be with us on Friday.

Wednesday I told them that the Prime Minister's people had earlier confirmed this interview several times but we were having trouble contacting them.

On Thursday I again stated that Mulroney was due tomorrow but I was beginning to feel he didn't have the guts to face my audience.

On Friday, without a word from the Prime Minister, he didn't show and we did a boisterous open line.

Until that Friday, we had done 2 ½ hours more on the NO side than the YES side because we calculated that Mulroney would come and thus even it all up as well as giving the YES people the last opportunity. To my considerable surprise the only complaint to the CRTC came from union leader Jack Munro who supported Charlottetown and whose nose was out of joint. This surprised me for I had always thought a lot of Jack and had never known him to whine. There were, to be fair, a great number of whiners including Peter C. Newman who, though only a BC resident for a very short time, wrote me and said, "For those of us British Columbians (!) who voted YES" I was being unfair in the amazingly little amount of gloating I did.

It's interesting to note that every constituency in BC (that's how the votes were counted) voted NO and almost all of them by about two-thirds to one-third.

What staggered me throughout was the abysmal ignorance of the YES people about BC and its feelings, a good example being Ian Haysom, then Editor of the Vancouver Sun. In his column the weekend after the vote he apologized for being so out of touch with the people! For the rest of the YES leaders the issue was airbrushed out of history, never to be discussed again. It will, however, re-assert itself and you can bet the ranch on that.

Interestingly, Bill Fox, who served as director of communications to Brian Mulroney, wrote a book on the Mulroney years and in the index there is one reference to Meech Lake and none on the Charlottetown Accord! It's rather like CKNW and me, but on a much larger scale: airbrush unpleasantness out of your history!

Just before the vote, Diane Francis, my editor at the Financial Post, phoned me and asked if it was really true that BC would vote NO.

I assured her that it was true.

She asked by what margin.

I replied 2/3-1/3.

She exclaimed that this sounded like a vote behind the late Iron Curtain.

In fact it was 68-32%.

Before leaving this subject, I want to mention two of my listeners and guests, retired schoolteachers **Bud and Monica Smith**, who had formed a group called Loyal British Columbians for Canada. Somehow this name was too close to another group's name and they were informed by

The Secretary of State's office that if they persisted they could go jail.

They didn't know what Bud (no relation to the
former BC Attorney-General) and Monica were
made of. They simply changed the name and
went to work. Starting from their small house in
Burnaby and their neighbours they eventually
had scores of people handing out pamphlets and
my editorials at ferry docks and other similar areas. After the vote, in my article for the Financial
Post, I summed up the referendum vote by saying, "It shows that in BC you don't mess around
with Bud and Monica Smith!"

My own reaction after the vote was one of re-
lief plus sorrow, as well as anger that the Prime
Minister could have put our federation through
such dangerous stress. In retrospect, it may have
been a good thing because millions of Canadians had seen the constitution from the inside out.
Any government that tries its inherent elitism out
on the Canadian public again will do so at their
peril, especially when one remembers that in the
election after the referendum, the Conservatives
were all but shut out with their MPs reduced to
two and with their Prime Minister, Kim Campbell, losing her own seat in the onslaught.

CHAPTER FIVE

Issues

THE ENVIRONMENT

I have long considered myself an environmentalist, but you be the judge.

In 1978-79 I was BC's Minister of Environment, during which I stopped the slaughter of wolves in the north, brought in a moratorium on exploration and mining of uranium and saved the lovely Skagit River, near Hope BC, from becoming a lake if the Seattle Light and Power Company (SLP) raised the Ross Dam.

Let's start with the issue of the Skagit River. The City of Seattle, which owned SLP, had the right to raise the Ross Dam under a 1941 agreement with the BC government. Nothing happened for the longest time but ever vigilant was a group, from all political persuasions, called ROSS for "Run Out Skagit Spoilers". In 1978 Seattle finally announced that it was going to raise the dam and it was on my watch. After full consideration I went to Premier Bill Bennett and said I simply couldn't see this happen under my jurisdiction. The Premier supported me and told me to settle the matter. It was one of my proudest moments in politics.

There was an amusing side of this. Seattle's Mayor, Charles Royer, refused to deal with a mere cabinet minister and demanded that he speak to the Premier. Protocol nixed that so my assistant, Tony Stark, arranged with Royer's executive assistant, his brother Bob, that we meet in an office next to the mayor's so he could listen and send in notes if needed!

Put simply, we made a deal whereby BC would give Seattle the power they would have lost.

I remember a couple of months later, fly rod in hand, I was on my favourite run on the Skagit saying to myself, "You've been an awful asshole in much of your life, but saving this was a plus for your chequered career."

It would be very wrong not to note the work of the Run Out Skagit Spoilers (ROSS) organization that made this an issue and kept it so for several years. ROSS was apolitical and included Dr. Tom Perry of the left and The Honourable John Fraser, a prominent Conservative MP and the Speaker of the House of Commons for many years. Without their work there might never have been a chance for me to get involved.

In writing about my role as an environmentalist on radio let me make it clear that I have little way of knowing how much, if any, impact my show, the editorials and guests, had on the outcome of crusades. That is for others to say. All I can tell you is that at the annual meeting of the Wilderness Committee in 2012, I was given the prestigious Eugene Rogers Award for my work trying to save the environment. That – plus the chance to work on the podium with Joe Foy, Gwen Barlee and Ben West of the Wilderness Committee – was a great honour.

Am I by this saying that I'm about to retire from the field of battle? I don't know. I'm in my 82nd year and physically, at any rate, feeling my years a bit.

This era is bringing an assault on the environment and social justice such as has never been seen before, in the sense of the number of places the assault is coming from and the seriousness of the issues. I must admit that there are times I get discouraged.

ALCAN AND THE NECHAKO RIVER

In the late 80s and early 90s I had been aware for some time of the Aluminum Company of Canada (Alcan) plan to lower the Nechako River near Prince George, BC, under what they called the Kemano Completion Project. I had done nothing while many, including my old friend Ben Meisner of CKPG in Prince George, were working their butts off opposing this scheme. Unfortunately, in terms of getting the mainstream media to get involved, they weren't making much progress.

Some background.

Back in the 1950s Alcan and the Provincial government made a deal where Alcan had the right to make enormous environmental changes, including turning a river around and creating a new lake, in order to create a lot of electric energy. In turn, Alcan would build an aluminum processing plant at Kitimaat on the BC north coast and sell its excess of energy into the grid. Indeed, underlying this whole issue was that making electricity was more profitable than making aluminum.

By the late 80s, Alcan wanted to create more electricity, which meant lowering the flow of the Nechako River, a critical route for Chinook and Sockeye salmon on their way to their spawning grounds in the Stuart Lake system.

In May of 1993 I was asked to do a show out of Terrace, BC, where my principal guest would be Bill Rich, a vice-president of Alcan. That interview was one of the worst of my career. I was utterly unprepared and lobbed one slow pitch after another.

When I got back to Vancouver I received a call from Ben Meisner, who had a powerful open line program at CKPG in Prince George. He was not known for mincing words and I heard, "Mair, that was the worst goddamn interview I have ever heard. You obviously know fuck-all about this Kemano project so I'm sending some stuff so you can learn something!"

And he did. And there were two main themes – the Kemano Completion Project, or Kemano II, was put together in secret under all but fraudulent circumstances and its completion would certainly wipe out salmon runs because the lowering of the Nechako would permit the river to become too warm for salmon to navigate. In the process, many fine scientists in the Department of Fisheries and Oceans had been retired, shunted aside or had simply quit in disgust. This was an enormous issue that simply didn't catch on with the populated areas of BC.

Upon reading the material Ben sent me, the first thing I did was arrange an on air debate between Bill Rich and Ben Meisner.

It was fascinating and damned good radio. Rich had all manner of statistics and Meisner the passion. From that moment on, it was a new ball game. My show became the focal point of the fight and the valiant folks who had been fighting Alcan had an outlet.

As an aside, Bill Rich, in a fit of pique, exclaimed, "Alcan's not in the aluminum business: it's in the power business!" This was against the original agreement both in fact and in spirit. Somehow this seminal confession did not catch media attention, hard as I tried to make that happen.

The local First Nations had had much of their territory flooded by Alcan in the 50s. Apparently the Carrier Sekani had, in the 50s, signed an agreement through the local Indian agent, which authorized Kemano I. But now the truth emerged – the document was all signed with Xs - all of which, it transpired, had been made by one person! One is compelled to think that that one person was the Indian agent himself, or someone in his office.

After the flooding, trappers came home to find their homes and graveyards and other sacred lands under water. It was a terrible thing and a shattering example of our attitude towards First Nations.

Kemano II was a three-way agreement between BC, Ottawa and Alcan – Indians and other interested parties were simply not consulted because the parties to the agreement were not in the slightest bit concerned with them and under the law of the time didn't have to be.

To make it all look good, a weekend meeting between the two governments and Alcan was chaired by Dr. David Strangway who was President of the University of British Columbia and, who, by his own admission, knew nothing about the issues. The scientific evidence accepted by all came from Alcan's pet poodles, Triton Engineers.

As the fight went on, retired DFO scientist Dr. Gordon Hartman guided me through the technical shoals. He was one of a number of former

DFO scientists who had all been shunted aside and were dubbed by Alcan as "the dissident scientists", a sobriquet they gladly bore. They were six in all, and they all gave evidence to the BC Utilities Commission in 1992. They were:

Dr. J. Harold Mundie, working with DFO at the time of the Lorna Barr/Larkin hearing. Harold is now deceased

Dr. Don Alderdice, DFO scientist, now deceased.

Bill Schouwenberg, DFO Management, in Vancouver

Dr. Cole Shirvell, DFO retired scientist. Now lives half time in New Zealand

Tom Brown, DFO Species at Risk Program, at the Pacific Biological Station, Nanaimo

Dr. Gordon Hartman, DFO retired scientist, living in Nanaimo

One of my most prized possessions is a large poster showing a salmon leaping up a falls, signed by all the "dissident scientists".

As matters progressed it was passion and anger amounting to a fight where the governments and Alcan had all the weapons – until I got a brown envelope from one of the "dissident scientists" which contained a study done by the DFO two years before the agreement was signed. I took the study home – it was a huge, unanimous condemnation of the project by the #1 team of fish scientists in the country. Without getting too deeply into science talk, the report said, in essence, that

the salmon runs passing through the Nechako were already in grave danger but that if the
Nechako were lowered further, it was only a matter of time before low water and high tempera-
tures would coincide and decimate these runs.

To have refused to consider this study then
keeping it secret was disgraceful.

This report had no role in the Strangway negotiations – neither did any of the scientists who
wrote it.

The Federal Fisheries Minister, Tom Siddon,
made it clear that this enterprise was a reasonable
"risk" and that politicians, not scientists, would
make the decision.

But this wasn't good enough anymore because
once a "risk" was admitted it was only common
logic that if you continue to run that risk, sooner
or later it becomes a reality.

The pressure on the BC government became
very heavy, especially since the Liberal leader,
Gordon Campbell, after looking at all my documents, started speaking out. Premier Mike Harcourt, in an ironic moment, asked the Public
Utilities Committee (BCUC) to look at the matter
– ironic because some years later Campbell, who
thought originally that using the BCUC was a
splendid idea, by now was Premier, became enraged by a BCUC ruling that annoyed him and
his government, and gutted it of most of its authority!

To keep a long story from getting longer, suffice it to say that the BCUC found against the Kemano II agreement and, to the horror of some and delighted surprise to others, Harcourt tubed it.

This caught me by surprise. Wendy and I were on our way to dinner and I was talking about the futility of the fight and we heard the news on the radio that it had been axed. Waiting for me at The Cheshire Cheese Restaurant at the Lonsdale Quay was BCTV, wanting to hear my very happy thoughts.

It had been an interesting time for me. I was starting to get muffled grumbles from Station management that I was spending too much time on the issue. That, however, is not how the public saw it, judging by the ratings.

I have often said since then that *you never know you've won until you win.*

Our show got the coveted Michener Award for our efforts.

In a delightful irony, the town of Terrace's Council had passed a by-law declaring that Terrace was a "Rafe Mair free zone" while the Mayor and Council of Hazleton presented me with a beautiful fly-rod! Terrace, you see, was on the coast and would have profitably sent men and equipment to the Kemano II project, while those on the other side of the mountains, like Hazleton, would have borne the brunt of the tragedy.

Many people asked me why we couldn't sue the government or Alcan and the answer may seem arcane but it's because the only people who can sue on a contract are those party to it. In fact, the town of Kitimaat brought a suit and got second prize for just that reason. In short, the agreement was between the two senior governments and Alcan and they are the only ones who have the "status" to sue to enforce an agreement they didn't want to happen. For the rest of us, the remedy is political – which is cold comfort indeed.

During all this, quite unintentionally, I got CKNW very pissed off at me.

I got a tip-off that Alcan was doing a massive advertising campaign to run in papers, TV and radio. I told the audience and speculated that it would be touchy-feely, with Bill Rich fly-fishing the Capilano River to simulate the Nechako. Evidently I came pretty close to the mark and Alcan cancelled the program – eliminating a healthy pay-off for CKNW!

The CKNW role was confirmed by a member of management and I was as popular as a skunk at a garden party.

A final note. In the middle of this scrap I was invited to speak at a Prince George Chamber of Commerce luncheon. Alcan had a table of ten, including their vice president of public relations Les Holroyd, right in front of the mic. Needless to say, I spoke on the Kemano II project and after my speech, opened the floor for questions. Not a peep from the Alcan table. Not a question. Nary a whisper. After the lunch ended, Holroyd and company rushed over to the TV and radio folk and denounced me and all I had said. I was given the opportunity to point out to the media that none of them had the guts to do that at the luncheon.

All bullies are cowards and this bunch proved that!

PITT RIVER GRAVEL PIT

On this issue, the main heroes were an environmental group called PRAWN, as well as Danny Gerak who owns and runs a fishing lodge on the Pitt River which has a number of very fishable tributaries and all have spawning areas (redds) for all species of Pacific salmon. The issue? A gravel pit was scheduled to open which would seriously threaten all the rivers.

For my trouble, Danny had my wife Wendy and me, fly rods in hand, flown to a tributary of the Pitt for a superb afternoon of fishing for Bull Trout, with a fish every other cast. It was a brilliant day and we were flown over the entire beautiful area, punctuated by a ride back right past the spectacular "Lions" into Vancouver. This was to stand me in good stead when, in 2008, I was invited to speak at a rally to save the Pitt from being ruined by an Independent Power plant.

In any event I got into the fight against the gravel operation. In consequence of the big overall fight – my role was minor - Premier Glen Clark banned the project but found another gravel mine for the company.

FISH FARMS

I first got wind of dangers posed by Atlantic salmon fish farms to wild salmon in 2001. The problem at first was simple: fish farms placed hundreds of thousands of farmed Atlantic salmon in cages along our coast and, because they needed water movement to wash out the farms, sited them near river mouths where wild salmon spawned and from which the smolts entered the ocean for their long voyage.

My first involvement came with news that these farmed fish were escaping in the thousands into the wild. With the incredible help from then-University of Alberta, now University of Victoria, fish biologist John Volpe, I was able to get chapter and verse as to what these escapees were doing. In the very little time and money he had, he could confirm that in three streams there were hundreds of escaped Atlantics.

There was no real fear that these escapees would breed with wild stock – it's doubtful if they can. What they were doing, however, was occupying the redds and displacing wild stock.

I interviewed John Van Dongen, Minister for Agriculture, Food and Fisheries in BC, who gives the term stubborn Dutchman a whole new meaning. Despite the massive evidence, Van Dongen maintained that only three escaped fish had got into our rivers. As he left my studio Van Dongen said that he couldn't understand why I was making such a stink as it wasn't a political issue.

"It will be, Minister," I said. "It will be."

A week or so later, Minister of Sustainable Resource Management, the late Stan Hagen, was on my show saying that Van Dongen was wrong and that only two escapees had been found in BC rivers, leaving me to refer to these half-wits as "Three fish Van Dongen" and "Two fish Hagen".

In the spring of 2001 I heard about Alexandra Morton and her work in the Broughton Archipelago.

Alex is a biologist from California who came to BC to study whales. She met a Canadian marine biologist and they married and in due course had a son.

One day, while her husband dived to install some sonar equipment to hear the whales, an unspeakable tragedy occurred. His equipment failed and in spite of Alex's heroic efforts he drowned right before her eyes and those of their young son.

We're talking about some plucky lady here!

One day some local First Nations people came to Alex and told her that they had never seen so many sea lice in their lives – could they have anything to do with diminished runs of Pink Salmon? Alex began to test and found large numbers of Pink smolts, trying to go to sea, infested with sea lice. To cut to the chase, fish pens with hundreds of thousands of hosts created millions of sea lice which preyed on the migrating Pacific smolts. Runs of salmon were hugely diminished.

The Department of Fisheries and Oceans (which is not only mandated to help salmon but is also mandated to *promote* fish farms!) threatened to arrest Alex for illegal testing.

Alex and I started doing shows on a regular basis and I started to editorialize against these farms. My show started a registry for restaurants that only served wild salmon and we encouraged people to eat there and for everyone to ask at any and all restaurants before ordering, whether or not they served wild salmon. (Interestingly, the Earl's restaurant chain defends their selling farmed salmon on the grounds that they are Pacific Chinooks. This is worse than Atlantic salmon because in addition to the other problems, they *can* breed with wild Chinook and thus weaken the species. Somehow the owner, "Bus" Fuller has trouble understanding that. I understand that Earl's and the restaurants they own have changed their policy to wild salmon only.)

Wendy and I quit going to Earl's Restaurants – where we had a welcome discount card - on this issue and we threatened to leave Ya Ya's restaurant in Horseshoe Bay if they continued to serve farmed salmon. Ya Ya's (Now Olive and Anchor) quickly changed and we dine there twice a week. As the proprietor Ricky Kim told us, fresh salmon was very good for business. We also encouraged Milestone's to change their policy – which they did on the slogan "Milestones is going wild!"

Soon after Alex and I started partnering our pitch she asked Wendy and me to visit her in Echo Bay where a supporter in Port McNeill would provide a boat.

We stayed in Port McNeill overnight and that evening Jennifer Lash from the Living Oceans Society warned me that we would be picketed the next morning by the Mayor, a tiresome windbag named Gerry Furney, and a massive demonstration. The citizens thought that if farmed fish went, their packing plant would go under.

The next morning at 6:30 we saw a huge crowd picketing the marina, led by the mayor using a loud hailer to heap insults at me. I won't deny it was scary. When Wendy and I were stopped at the entrance to the marina I asked the man if he was really going to prevent us from going out on a boat. He was silent for a moment then said, "No, Mr. Mair, I can't do that," and let us past to the boos of the rest of the gang, very much joined by the Mayor.

It turned out to be a wonderful tour with Alex and First Nations folks describing what we were seeing.

It only reinforced a recent experience of mine, while fishing in Sechelt inlet in front of a fish farming area, where I caught a cutthroat which was covered with lice – they stood out like raisins on a bun.

WHERE I BLEW IT

Let's look at an environmental issue that became huge and that I simply buggered up on – the so-called Run of Rivers policy where BC Hydro was forced to buy all the power private companies generated.

I had, over the years, interviewed David Austin, lawyer for the Independent Power Producers (IPPs) many times and simply did not ask the right questions. It was one slow pitch after another. As I had on Kemano II, I accepted the bullshit I was hearing.

One day, when I was in my very short-lived career as an internet broadcaster, I had Austin on and fed him the usual soft pitches. After the show I was reamed out by my producer whom I had only just met. He spelled out just what these so-called "run of river" projects were all about. I have not named him because he asked me not to but let's just say he was absolutely right and I had been a blind asshole (my epithet, not his!).

In 2008, when Tom Rankin, who ran Save Our Rivers Society, asked me to speak at a public meeting on putting IPP dams on tributaries of the Pitt, I agreed. I was informed and ready. During 2008 and until after the 2009 election I was on contract with Tom, who spent a hell of a lot of his own money in the fight. Since September 20, 2009, I've been heavily involved since in The Common Sense Canadian, an environmental website (www.thecanadian.org) which I co-founded with the brilliant documentary maker, Damien Gillis, dealing vigorously with so called "run of river" projects.

But I was late into the fight and I'm ashamed of myself. I've done the best I can to atone for my error in the 2009 Provincial election and since.

FIRST NATIONS

Like most BC kids I learned next to nothing about local Indians. What we learned was the history of the Iroquois, Huron and Algonquin tribes – all Eastern tribes. For example, I had no idea that there were more than 30 separate languages in our local Indian population. I knew nothing of the history of our aboriginal population, their customs, laws and culture.

There were no Indians in the schools I attended and the only Indian I knew was Alfred Scow who was a classmate of mine in Law School. I fished on the Musqueam Reserve in Vancouver but didn't get to know any of the members.

When I was in government the Calder decision came down, which started the Federal government's prodding of BC into recognizing Indian title to land not subject to a treaty.

Delgamuuk came on the scene and the sum of it and other cases was that First Nations did indeed not only have an interest in non-treaty lands but that much of it they owned outright.

I opposed the Nisga'a treaty only because of constitutional problems I saw that it created.

When I was in Kamloops I got to know First Nations and their leaders and when in government I negotiated the issue of Indian land needed to build a bridge over the North Thompson.

In my media career I learned about the terrible injustices heaped upon First Nations over the years.

My learning curve was steep but I came to the point I am now – supportive of aboriginal claims. Whatever I thought of constitutional concerns are, by reason of court decisions, moot and I've never been much for fighting just for the sake of fighting. I go further and say I now accept that these decisions were right.

I have come a hell of a long way and I can only hope that our education system now teaches what I should have learned but didn't.

At my Roast for my 80th birthday, Grand Chief Stewart Philip and two colleagues, Chief Marilyn Baptiste and Chief Bob Chamberlin, were very kind to me and it was one of my greatest moments, one I will always cherish.

It was a long journey but I'm glad to be where I am.

CHAPTER SIX

Life on the Media Stage

MY ROLE AS THE BROADCASTER

Many have asked and continue to ask what all these issues have to do with broadcasting. Shouldn't the broadcaster be even-handed or perhaps even neutral?

First off, there is a difference between a newscaster and a talk show host. I have never considered myself a "journalist" in the traditional sense. I'm an editorialist. This means the listener needs to know what the broadcaster is all about before he/she can properly evaluate where the questions and environmental mutterings are coming from.

Judging a broadcaster's politics is difficult at the best of times, since if he is doing the job properly he is holding the government's feet to the fire regardless of which political party is in charge and regardless of what the issues may be. I did that with Bill Bennett, Bill Vander Zalm, Rita Johnston, the four premiers the NDP had between 1991-2001, and the two Liberal premiers since.

In my own case I was only even-handed in the sense that I gave all sides a chance to speak their minds. How the hell could I do hard hitting editorials to open the show then tread gingerly when those issues were raised on my show?

I have changed over the years to the extent that I've moved from the centre to centre left. I believe in the market place but I can't think of a major company or a government that I believe has told the truth. Having been in government, I know how much bullshit they peddle and the high paid flacks they use to help them.

During my time in government I watched and I still watch the crap peddled by companies who, while devastating the environment, solemnly swear they aren't and that they love the out-of-doors with a passion. They lie, cheat and buy politicians who are often so thick they don't understand that they have been bought and paid for, and I refer you back to fish farms and ministers Van Dongen and Hagen.

I don't trust big labour either, although the last 10 years or so have been hard on them because of the bad times. I have an ongoing feud with Jim Sinclair of the BC Federation of Labour and his predecessor, and now president of the Canadian Federation of Labour, Ken Georgetti, over the secret vote for joining a union. Somehow they claim that under the present secret ballot system, management puts pressure on workers but that with an open vote the Union would not! How "democrats" can deny democracy's most sacred principle, the secret ballot, is beyond me. Still and all, I support unions.

Labour has a long and valuable history and while they have lost the power they once had they still have new battles to fight such as a better minimum wage, better working conditions, better representation of those who lack the power to help themselves.

I don't trust big "charities". I had a long association with the Canadian Mental Health Society which amongst other things confirms that whoever takes the Queen's shilling does the Queen's bidding, and this applies to most if not all private organizations that get government funding.

WHAT HAS HAPPENED TO THE MEDIA?

When I was in government we had, to say the least, an aggressive media. Some of the names come quickly to mind – Jack Webster, Pat Burns, Gary Bannerman, Marjorie Nichols, Jim Hume, Jack Wasserman, Barbara McClintock, Andy Stephen, Dave Abbott, Dave Todd, Allan Garr and the list goes on. We never had a moment's peace but it made us a better government.

Media vigilance continued with Vander Zalm and the NDP years but the Provincial Liberals have all but had a free ride.

For example, I don't recall a single critical article by leading local columnists on fish farms, independent power producers, pipelines and tankers up until this moment – December 2013. I exempt from that list Mark Hume, who writes for the Toronto Globe and Mail. But think on that. Compare the coverage given Glen Clark's problems about the neighbour who wanted a gambling licence or the fast ferries issue. Vaughn Palmer and Mike Smyth – especially the former - were all over them, but not a peep for 13 years on the issues I mentioned!

In fact it goes to the root of our written and unwritten constitutional protections we give the media. For by not questioning the government they must be taken to approve its actions.

The editor of the editorial pages of the Sun is a "Fellow" of the far right wing "think tank", the Fraser Institute. Is it simply accidental that, for example, Op Ed pieces by fish farmers appear with great regularity with none opposing? The same thing with private power. And with pipelines and tanker traffic. And the Agriculture Land Reserve.

Local writers have, in the Postmedia papers, been replaced by writers from other papers, the syndication fee obviously being less than a local writer would cost.

The big environmental issues of the day –

loss of farmland, loss of wildlife preserves, fish farms, private power (which has bankrupted BC Hydro) pipelines and tanker traffic attract no news stories of any consequence let alone editorial attention, a deficiency that the publishers refuse to comment upon.

On one occasion, after I criticized the Vancouver Province, its managing editor, Wayne Moriarty called me at home in near tears. "Rafe, do you think I tell my columnists what to write and what not to write?" he asked.

"Wayne," I replied, "you don't have to."

In British Columbia, the major newspapers – The Vancouver Sun, The Province and the Victoria Times Colonist – are all owned by the same company, Postmedia (formerly Canwest), which also owns a large number of community papers. Those they don't own are all mostly controlled by the far right-winger, David Black. It's the same with television. All of these papers either support all government decisions or, by their silence, accept them uncritically.

I have been fired by so many radio stations and newspapers I've lost count. Free speech in Canada means dissenting nicely within the accepted boundaries – I'll get into that more a bit further on.

I'm not complaining – I've done well by the media. The question that ought to bother citizens is why was I fired? It certainly was not because of loss of listeners!

I actually fired a newspaper, the Vancouver Province. Here's how it happened.

I had been writing a column in the Province for some years and I was getting a bit antsy from criticism by management on my editorial subjects. One morning I learned that The Ottawa Citizen, also owned by Canwest, (now Postmedia) had fired its editor Russell Mills because either he made a speech his bosses didn't like or he did an editorial without CanWest's permission – both versions have currency.

Gordon Gibson, who then wrote for the National Post, a Canwest paper, did a column deploring this attack on free speech. His column was spiked and I was so damned mad I fired the Province on air saying that I, too, deplored this sort of fascism, that I didn't want to write for this sort of paper and suggested that listeners who felt the same way should cancel their subscriptions.

The Sun, a Canwest paper, was enraged and demanded that their PR flack have equal time on air but *not* on the Rafe Mair Show. Bill Good, who shuns controversy like a dose of clap, said he wouldn't do it because he "had friends on both sides"!

The next choice was Jon McComb, a first class broadcaster who methodically tore the poor man to bits. It was brutal. I admired it so much I ran it the next morning on my show and said that this interview should be compulsory listening for all journalism students.

CanWest phoned the owners of CKNW saying that they would drop all ads and also withdraw from civic projects in which they were both involved unless I was canned. Management declined their offer.

I'm told that a great many subscriptions were cancelled.

As I'm sure you're detecting, I despise the establishment in this country, which has a line of dissent over which no one can stray. This accounts for the fact that Stevie Cameron (the best journalist in the country), Claire Hoy, Andrew MacIntosh, Rick Salutin – and Rafe Mair – no longer write for or broadcast in mainstream media.

WHAT DO THEY LEARN IN JOURNALISM SCHOOLS?

It's instructive to look at what the media financed journalism teaches – in fact the blue ooze of the Establishment has crept into journalism schools. Big time. Let me share with you this story.

Some years ago I received a call from a young woman from the Ryerson School of Journalism – one of the top journalism schools in the country - who asked me to do the lead article for their Annual. I agreed and waived any fee. She needed it within ten days and within seven I sent them an article on "free speech". I closed by saying that "Journalism students wanting to work in the mainstream media would either self-censor or be censored".

Several weeks passed and the young woman called again to tell me that my article was "unsuitable".

"Was it badly written?"

"No," it is very well written but unsuitable."

"Unsuitable to whom, and why?" I asked.

"It's just unsuitable but we have a couple of options – we'll pay you $100 or you can write another for us that is suitable."

"No," I said, "there's a third option – you can all go fuck yourselves."

Talk about "suspicions confirmed".

In the summer of 2011 I received a note from another young woman from Ryerson wanting to know what was my biggest disappointment in the media? Apparently Ryerson was surveying journalists all over the country. We made a date to meet in Lions Bay where I live. A day or so later I received an email in advance of the interview asking what this big disappointment was, so I said, "When Ryerson spiked my column on free speech."

The appointment was cancelled and this was followed by a note saying that the subject I had chosen was not within the purview of what they were looking for. But, she said, this cancellation had nothing to do with my previous dealings with the university.

Where would they have got that idea!!!

Free speech and freedom of the press are in our constitution – do we have free speech in reality? Was A.J. Liebling right when he said, "Freedom of the press is guaranteed only to those who own one".

Is there a limit to be placed on on-air criticism?

I say, yes there is. And it's simply that which the audience imposes by either listening or not.

Does management have the right to judge on air criticism?

Of course it does, and can do so capriciously for they own the station. The point is that they *shouldn't* and listeners (thus consumers of advertised products) should punish them if they do. To deprive broadcasters of free speech will lead to milquetoast radio that only milquetoasts listen to. And we have an example in Vancouver in CKNW, which now has dropped by about 50% since I left and "pablum radio" started.

The bigger question is this - should criticism in general have any limits?

In a free speech society, no. The penalty for free speech that "goes too far" is lack of credibility.

I start with a basic assumption - everyone puts their own spin on what they say. In ordinary social intercourse this poses no problem because we all discount that which we feel is excessive. To a broadcaster, accepting what he is told, uncritically, betrays an inability to do what the public hasn't the time or inclination to do for itself - separate the pepper from the fly shit.

My standard was and remains simple - when it comes from governments or businesses or indeed any public body including unions, I don't believe a word of it. Not a word. It's in the interest of governments and industry to put their best foot forward - the former to get or retain votes, the latter to make money. This is their natural state, what they do for a living, so to speak. Only the terminally naive would believe uncritically the pronouncements of the mighty. If they were actually telling you the entire truth, why would they employ large public relations departments and pay enormous sums to private flacks to tell them how to "sell" their products? Or cover up their mistakes, even evil mistakes. We seem to lose sight of the fact that the only reason for a corporation is to make money and the principal if not only raison d'être for a politician is to get re-elected. To gild the lily or worse comes naturally.

There should be no limitations on the search for truth, wartime being an exception.

Unhappily, the media in general has found a way to stifle free speech, called self-censorship. It's practiced throughout all media and has turned tough talk or writing into meaningless mush. Governments and advertisers now have the upper hand because the media generally is in terrible fiscal shape. When I was broadcasting a station could ignore the feelings of government and advertisers. No more.

The plain truth is that writers and broadcasters self-censor because if they don't they don't get published or near a microphone. They have families to support and for all of us that comes first. Thus has the media fallen into the hands of the "right", leaving the expression of free speech to the blogger on the internet, which itself gets closer and closer to being controlled by government.

A final note.

Back in 2001, with some help from Jimmy Pattison, I set up a scholarship at the UBC School of Journalism and I was asked to make the presentation. I did so and told the assembled students my views on free speech in the media.

It's an annual scholarship and I've never been invited back to present my own scholarship!

That blue ooze of the Establishment and the media they control has deeply penetrated our schools of Journalism, for God's sake!

Free speech in Canada?

You must be kidding!

THE WORST DECISIONS I MADE

Let's start with Iraq.

I tried very hard to make good judgment on this and failed horribly.

The question was a simple one – did Saddam Hussein have weapons of mass destruction or didn't he?

On the "yes" side were President Bush, Tony Blair and Colin Powell. On the "no" side were Hans Blix, the UN inspector, Scott Ritter, who also was a UN inspector and the UN Security Council save the US and Britain.

It was a very serious question since Saddam had used missiles against Israel in the Gulf War not, thank God, with nuclear warheads. He had shown no hesitation in gassing Kurds in the northern part of Iraq and made no secret of his hatred of Israel.

Whom to believe?

I wouldn't believe Bush's statement on anything but I did trust Blair because politically, he had a lot to lose. I also believed Powell, for until we found out later that he could lie with the worst of them, he seemed so honest and credible.

I backed the wrong horses.

In my defence I must say that I didn't support them from any philosophical reason but from evaluating the "players" then making a judgment.

I did make a serious error in judgment in deciding not to interview Scott Ritter, an inspector who had written a book on the subject called **Endgame: Solving the Iraq Crisis.** Not to have interviewed Mr. Ritter was simply stupid and way outside my rule of interviewing every person involved in an issue.

I don't know why I blew it but I did and I have no excuse.

I mentioned earlier that I also blew it with the so-called "run of river" and again have little excuse.

I was not up to speed on energy matters and

started interviews with David Austin, lawyer for the Independent Power companies (IPPS) over hydro-electric power and BC Hydro. BC Hydro announced that they would license IPPs to produce electricity from rivers where there were "no appreciable fish values". In the absence of any credible voices to the contrary, I accepted their statement.

Bad Mistake. I suppose I had not yet reached the point I'm at now – I don't believe anything any government or corporation says. The idea I received from Austin's half dozen or more interviews was that these were "Mom and Pop" developments and just as they were described by Hydro and the Government.

I don't fault Austin – I was new to the issue and my questions were slow pitches. Then Finance Minister, Colin Hansen, did an interview for a Liberal blog which said all the things Austin did and I was dumb enough to accept what he had to say because he seemed like such a decent man and so honourable. They both were extremely economical with the truth.

I didn't have the scales fall from my eyes until 2008 when the Pitt River issue, discussed elsewhere, came on the screen.

I can only offer the feeble excuse that no one else seemed to see what was happening – at least no one came forward. As with the Kemano II issue I should have smelled a rat.

As with Kemano II, I can only say that I was in the fight after I "saw the light" but how much different it might have been if my audience was offered more than what I gave them and sooner.

CHAPTER SEVEN

People Along the Way

I have no idea how many 1000s of people I have interviewed. Some impressions, however, have stuck out in my mind. I have sorted these out not in any order of importance but rather in nationality, namely Canadian, American or British.

CANADA

I first met **Preston Manning** just after he became the leader of the Reform Party and I quickly knew that here was a man whose economic views wouldn't come close to according with mine but that his real strength was his zeal to reform the way Canada governed itself.

In the 1993 election I arranged for him to be a panellist of a presentation of the Canadian Real

Estate Board at a meeting I'd been hired to chair. These realtors, mostly from Toronto, had never heard of the man but were much impressed by what they heard.

When, after the 1997 election the Reform Party replaced the Tories then became the Official Opposition in the election following, I was not surprised.

Preston Manning suffered from the "Stanfield trauma", namely a decent guy who couldn't win the big one. Sadly, opening up the leadership of the party and losing it to Stockwell Day, who then lost it to Stephen Harper killed the party. It was then that many Canadians, even in Central Canada, began to see what a mistake they had made in casting Preston Manning aside. Manning left a legacy of reforms in the political arena. I suppose, over the years, I interviewed him a dozen times or more. He answered the tough questions – and any leader of a right wing party faces those – and never tried to run out the clock. He left, in my opinion, a positive legacy that will live even though he never achieved power.

I first interviewed **Kim Campbell,** our former Prime Minister, when she was on the Vancouver School Board then as a Socred backbencher, then as a federal Justice Minister and finally as Prime Minister. It was under her federal responsibilities that we had the most sparks.

We had a great time dealing with constitutional issues such as Meech Lake and Charlottetown.

What was so good about it was that we both knew our briefs and the result was, I believe, both entertaining and informative. I also believe that the debates educated the public sufficiently so that when the referendum on the Charlottetown Accord came around, the public understood the issues thoroughly. That meant that the line of mindless, silly bullshit Joe Clark and Brian Mulroney were peddling just didn't wash. Ironically that was in part due to the fact that Kim dealt with the seriousness of the matter that the Clark/Mulroney simplistic platitudes papered over with mindless BS.

In saying that, I don't wish to put down Kim in any way. She did what a good minister should do – deal with the issues seriously and in depth. It wasn't her fault that the government lost the referendum ... it was clearly the fault of Brian Mulroney with the ultimate deadly irony that it was Kim Campbell, not Lyin' Brian, who paid the political forfeit.

I also remember Kim that when the Charlottetown debate got nasty she publicly reminded us all that we were all Canadians and that we should remember that we all had to live together when the vote was behind us.

Responsible and timely.

Carl Brewer was a fine if not great hockey player and **Susan Foster**, his partner, one very gutsy lady.

Over the years, the owners of the National Hockey League had stolen huge sums of money from the Players Pension Fund, set up in the 40s to take care of players, many of whom had been pressured into forfeiting higher education, to play hockey. Moreover, they played when salaries were infinitesimal and when injuries shortened or ended a career – too bad. What the owners had done was simple theft – they took the interest the pension plan earned and pocketed it. When the players challenged this fraud the owners decided to "money whip" them with high-powered lawyers and endless court procedures that eventually went to the Supreme Court of Canada. Carl Brewer and his fighting consort fought the owners without money, courage being the best they could bring to the fight and they had lots of that.

The media, with but one or two exceptions – Bruce Dowbiggan being a lonely Canadian exception and, may I immodestly say later joined by Rafe Mair – either pretended the issue wasn't there or openly supported crooks like Alan Eagleson who had two-timed the players he represented.

The players won in the Supreme Court of Canada and the owners still dragged their heels by saying that to compute the damages was too complicated. It wasn't too complicated to steal, just too complicated to count and make amends.

Because I had joined the fight in Vancouver I met with and had numerous phone and personal conferences with Carl and Susan during which I joked with Brewer that I was even prepared to forgive him for being a Maple Leaf.

Tragically, Carl died before he got much benefit from the wars he led but he left a legacy of enormous courage, which courage might not have been there had he not had the partner he did.

I learned from Carl, incidentally, that the players disliked Gordie Howe because he signed so cheaply and his salary was the benchmark for other players. The same was said about Maurice Richard and given what came later, they were right.

Carl Brewer and Susan Foster – true Canadian heroes.

Speaking of courage – I give you **Stevie Cameron**.

I declare my interest – Stevie Cameron is a friend of mine whom I've admired for a very long time, not the least for giving the Canadian Establishment the finger and suffering for it. Stevie is perhaps best remembered for *On The Take*, a chronicle of the Mulroney years, and *The Last Amigo* which sets out the Airbus Scandal starring Karl Heinz Schreiber and Brian Mulroney. Since this is a sketch, not a book in itself, let me confine myself to one incident – the admission by Brian Mulroney that, shortly after leaving office, he took $300,000 in cash from Karlheinz Schreiber, the acknowledged Mr. Fixit of the Airbus scandal who desperately fought extradition to Germany to face fraud charges. He lost.

The bags of cash story appeared in a rather unusual way.

On 31 Oct 2007 Edward Greenspon, editor of the Toronto Globe and Mail in his weekly column, on page 2, disclosed the bags of money issue and told how Mulroney tried to get him to kill the story promising that if he did, he, Mulroney would give him an even better one!

Then, in the same column, there was an attack on Stevie Cameron which alleged that she was a paid RCMP informer during the time she was collecting evidence for her books.

That Stevie, as all reporters dealing regularly with the police do, exchanged tidbits of information was never denied. Not only is this a common practice, even if it weren't reporters have the same obligation to report criminal acts as we the public do. The part that hurt was the statement that Stevie was a registered paid informant as if that somehow tainted the evidence she had collected for her books which was patently not true.

To me Stevie is the best journalist in the country, kept out of the mainstream press because she calls it like it is and the establishment of this country can't handle that.

Mike Harcourt is, to say the least, an interesting man. Affable and fun to be with, it's easy to see how people elected him to lead and then were disappointed. Not a natural New Democrat, he was appalled when the scandal involving Dave Stupich and what became Nanaimogate finally broke its bounds. Though utterly uninvolved in the matter, Harcourt handled it badly and felt constrained to resign which he did – leaving us with Glen Clark and the Fast Ferries fiasco,

A man of great personal courage given his nasty fall which could have killed him or left him paralyzed for life, he is also a great collector of sinecures.

I must also say that when I saw George Vancouver's grave in Petersham near London and what neglected condition it was in, and I so advised then Mayor Harcourt, the grave was promptly taken care of.

As a guest on air, he was the best I ever saw at running out the clock. Thus, when he came on my show during the Charlottetown Accord - he was BC Premier at the time - I had my producers book him for two hours because while I knew he could tap dance for an hour I didn't think he could go longer. I was right, in the second hour he got crucified by the callers.

He "wrote" a book which I haven't read because I simply refuse to read "as told to" books. I understand that there are lots of references to me, none flattering. On the premise that all publicity is good publicity I should thank him.

In fact, in my books Mike Harcourt is a helluva good guy – just a lousy premier, unsuitable to the position which is not necessarily a bad thing to be. The Peter Principle – "in a hierarchy, one is promoted until he reaches his level of incompetence" sums up Mike's political career.

Glen Clark is a man of ambition and a bright

guy. His trouble was that he had lousy judgment. He was always a good interview and privately a very gracious host.

I had one off air incident which has never been told. In 1997 I was asked by Premier Clark and Attorney-General Andrew Petter how I would deal with the "Calgary Accord", a brash way for the first ministers to avoid the people and bring in the provisions of the Charlottetown Accord in through the back door. The government was in a bind – if they refused the Opposition would paint them as "bad Canadians" but if they supported it, the people would skin them alive.

I suggested that they love the thing to death by putting in some "motherhood" clauses which while appearing to be helpful, would ensure its death.

The Clark government did that and that was the last anyone would hear about it again!

The "fast ferries fiasco" was his baby and he went ahead against all advice, some of which even came from friendly quarters. His downfall came over the gambling issue where a neighbour, who happened to be seeking a gambling license, did some work – for free – for Mr. Clark. It was just plain stupid and from the outset I asked "how could any senior politician be such a damned fool?"

When I was in charge of liquor under Bill Bennett, W.A.C. Bennett gave me great advice, "Rafe …don't ever meet with liquor people without someone with you." And he was dead right. Clark, by having a friendly relationship with a man wanting a gambling license, committed political suicide.

Too bad, because if he'd had good advice and had listened to it, he might still be Premier. I thought the charges against him were ill-considered and after the Crown had finished its case, I said, "it reminds me of that Peggy Lee favourite, *Is That All There Is?*"

That he landed a good job with Jimmy Pattison and has done brilliantly doesn't surprise me.

Marc Lalonde was, in the Trudeau era, a very powerful minister and was often touted as Trudeau's successor. He was a nice enough chap with a sunny appearing disposition but arrogant as hell. I got to know Marc during the exercise in patriating the constitution as we were both members of the Cabinet ministers group to try to find common ground and come up with recommendations for the "First Ministers".

As I mentioned, Marc was a tad on the arrogant side. We became squash partners and he was a much better player than I. When I would hit a bad shot just waiting to be converted into a point for him, Lalonde would exclaim "you fool" as he racked up another point.

In squash, if you are impeded by the other player, you're expected to cry out "let" thus stopping the game to be started again. This is so to avoid the player in the way getting hit by the ball.

One day after a particularly bad day for "you fool" I saw Marc, back to me, standing in front of me. I drilled him right in the ass calling "let" a spilt second after I made the shot. The squash ball, though soft, is traveling at about 200 miles an hour and if it hits you it not only hurts, it leaves a lovely bruise.

For some reason I was never able to get Marc to play another game!

Paul Martin Jr was, to me, a man who was so bound to the Canadian Establishment that he simply couldn't escape it. When he became Prime Minister he refused to come on my show in the event that it would produce bad sound bites that would echo across the nation.

Martin knew that there was discontent in BC and the platitudes he must spew forth in order to run out the clock wouldn't have done with me as host.

The following true story led to a permanent rift between Bill Good and me. I can't blame Bill because while accurate, I was a bit nasty.

At the end of my show, my job was to tell the audience what was coming up. And I should tell you that I was very cross with management because politicians didn't like coming on my show so they always opted for Good who was putty in their hands. Thus the federal Liberal government was programming the station or at least a large part of it.

On this occasion I said "coming up on the Bill

Good Show is Finance Minister Paul Martin who hasn't got the guts to come on this show and answer real questions".

Thereafter Mr. Martin and other prominent cabinet ministers came on my show.

It had an interesting side story.

In November of 2003 I received the Bruce Hutchison Lifetime Achievement Award at the annual Jack Webster dinner. The MCs were Bill Good and Pamela Martin. It was the biggest audience of all time at more than 1000. When I received the award I made a short speech which was followed by a spontaneous standing ovation - not quite unanimous as Bill refused to stand and pulled Pamela down as she started to get up. Or so I was informed.

When Bill received an honour in the following year at the Websters I tried to stand up and cheer but Wendy pulled me back! I would have been the only one and it would have been a sort of pay back.

Paul Watson is the founder and until early 2013 president of the Sea Shepherd Society. As this is written, Paul has just left the Sea Shepherd Society.

A certified Marine Captain, Paul is a hero of mine. He tried, as a lifetime endeavour, to save the mammals of the sea and did so against very heavy odds indeed.

Utterly fearless, Captain Watson once broadcast to me from a few miles off the Soviet Union coast where he was being chased by the Soviet navy and buzzed by their air force. It was high drama and nothing like what I'd done or have done since. It was one of those crackling sea to shore "over" calls which made what was a pretty harrowing experience all the more so by style of the call. The event giving rise to the interview was he had gone ashore on Kamchatka and destroyed a mink farm that used whale meat for feed.

His principal, though by no means only concern, was the world's whale population still, in this day and age, sought for food by Japan that pretends it uses them for scientific research where in fact it becomes sushi. On another front, the Faroe Islands, Paul stopped their annual kill of pilot whales done for the simple joy of killing them. I was in Faroe in 2011 and noted that on the back of one of their bank bills is an etching of a man clubbing a whale to death. My hunch is that the Faroese have returned to their disgusting practice now that Paul's gone.

Captain Watson is also active in the fight against seal hunts.

Of considerable interest, I think, is how, after harassing Peruvian authorities over environmental abuses of the Galapagos, he became partnered with the government in their protection.

I'm proud indeed to be a friend and a Member of the Board of Advisors of the Sea Shepherd Society I interviewed **Steve Fonyo**, who like Terry Fox had lost a leg to cancer and who was starting to complete Terry's run.

Again no one else was interested. Steve kept in touch with us nearly every evening and came on my show first when he returned.

I feel badly about how Steve's life went after he returned. He wasn't made of the same stuff Terry was and couldn't handle the situation. This was aggravated by the fact that the media and many if not most people, resented what Steve had done because he did what Terry was not able to do.

Steve got into trouble with alcohol and other drugs at the root of it, and I think it was very wrong to have taken his Order of Canada away from him. It's OK for a former Prime Minister to commit perjury and accept money that was to all accounts a bribe, but a gutsy kid who performed a near miracle misbehaves and gets dinged.

The Order of Canada has strange rules and priorities.

Vicki Gabereau is a superb broadcaster and well loved by Canadians from coast to coast. She provided me with a hall of fame "gotcha".

Back in the early 80s Vicki published a book of her recollections and the Vancouver Sun asked me to do a review of it. I did and I trashed it. No sooner had I sent it in I realized I was far too harsh but the Sun would have none of that and published it. I was scared stiff of what she would say if we ever met.

Well, we met on a number of social occasions and she couldn't have been nicer. I kept waiting for the other shoe to drop. Around 1992 Vicki left her TV show to go back into radio and she was, to my surprise, a guest on my show.

I kept fearing the worst but nothing happened.

Then it was a minute to go and I was starting to wind down and Vicki said, "Wait a minute, Rafe." And then she reamed me out good and proper for the book review. She knew she would get the last word because time was up. All I could say was that this was the most skilled "gotcha" I had ever known. And it was. I had to compliment her in the seconds left in the show and afterwards.

Was I angry?

Hardly – I was relieved it was finally over.

And we are on the very best of terms. It was a grand moment.

My involvement with CJOR/600AM had a lot to do with **Jimmy Pattison**, BC's own billionaire who owned both AM CJOR and its successor, 600AM.

Many years after leaving CJOR, I asked if 600AM – the successor to CJOR but now an old folks' music station – would be interested in me returning to start a talk show. Jimmy simply said that he would have his manager, Gerry Siemens give me a call. I took Siemens to lunch at the Vancouver Club and he wasn't interested. Worst of all, I got stuck with the lunch tab!

He eventually changed his mind, but my return to 600AM was not a successful one. My producer and pal Shiral Tobin and I were misfits in a station that sounded like it was owned by the ghosts of Frank Sinatra, Dean Martin and Sammy Davis Jr. The real problem with 600AM, which Pattison agreed with at a dinner with my agent, Red Robinson and me, is that you have to have compatible programming both before and after the talk show to make it work. I opened up and closed to the dulcet tones of the Rat Pack.

That the station went belly up not long after I left shows that they just didn't know anything about programming, except letting someone who has the personality of a warthog in heat push buttons from which music emerges.

After I left 600AM, this time amicably, at least for public consumption, I got a call from Jimmy saying he was sorry it happened, but that he left those decisions up to local management. He did promise Wendy and me a week in Palm Desert in Frank Sinatra's former home. We declined. I hold the distinction of having been fired twice by billionaire, Jimmy Pattison.

I had known Jimmy's reputation as a tough boss. It was said – and Jimmy later told me it was true – that when he first ran a car business, at the end of the month he would fire the salesman who had the fewest sales. Jimmy later told me that if there were extenuating circumstances like illness or a death in the family, he took that into account and did nothing.

"But Rafe," he told me, "I did the man no favour keeping him on if he was no good."

I got to know Jimmy a bit better over the years

as I was, from time to time, invited out on a cruise on his immense yacht, the *Nova Spirit*. I also had lunch with him occasionally because we had come to like one another.

An evening on Jimmy's yacht was interesting. He usually put people together with a plan obviously in mind. Often times I found myself on board with people I didn't like and who didn't like me. As you might suspect, Jimmy enjoyed seeing what happened. We were also all expected to say a few words on who we were and what we did – we sort of sang for our supper, so to speak.

At the end of the day, my favourite cliché. I like Jimmy but I'd like him even better if he paid me the $3500 he stiffed me when 600 AM fired me!

Pierre Berton was a great writer and I don't qualify that by Canadian – he was a great writer, period.

He was also a world class asshole full of himself to the exclusion of all others as any who gave him signing opportunity will attest. He was arrogant, demanding and unreasonable.

I had two brushes with Berton, one in studio and one that didn't happen.

The one that happened was at CJOR600 in the 80s when I interviewed him for a new book. He kept interrupting me to say "you should be asking me about this" or "let's move on to this". Being a stubborn SOB with 15 years' experience in examining witnesses I was mad as hell and vowed I would never interview him again.

Now I must say it here: I would and did interview a lot of people I didn't care for, including the Grand Wizard of The Ku Klux Klan, a hateful excuse for a human being, and Berton was the only one I blackballed. Sort of.

In the mid-90s Berton returned to town to flog a book and did a signing in a local book store in which one of my step daughters worked and she, a Berton fan, was completely flummoxed as she and the entire staff had to meet every petty instruction the great man gave including sharp pencils for his notebook, for whatever use that was.

He was scheduled to do my morning show, and when I found out I was livid though I couldn't and didn't blame my producers. It was a natural.

He was due for the last half hour and at 11:15 my senior producer came into my studio to say that Berton had just come from another radio station – a rival station, which was a no-no and had been even before my time.

Did his agent know about this rule? Yes she did but thought that the great Pierre would be an exception. He wasn't and I gave an unmistakable order: "Fuck him."

So that poor Shiral, my long-suffering and first class producer, had to go down to the waiting room and translate that message into something more polite. Which she did and Berton evidently had a hissy fit.

So in fact my second brush with Pierre Berton didn't happen.

Let me deal with two of Nova Scotia's greatest in one shot. I speak of **Anne Murray** and **Rita McNeil**.

I'm going to pass over Anne lightly because it was a pretty ordinary interview. I have long been a fan and that might have dulled my sabre. She has had a great career and my reaction was rather sexist I'm afraid – she was nudging 60 and she looked 35.

The late Rita McNeil reached her moment of truth at Expo '86 in Vancouver where her show brought them in by droves. She was in her mid-forties (a year older than Murray) and this was her breakthrough, after which she became very popular. For some reason she was especially popular in New Zealand, a country I have visited 25 times to fish and where I have dear friends and relatives, all of whom, it seems, are Rita fans.

It was Rita the person that fascinated me as much as her music. She was, to say the least, not pretty, and she had far from the perfect body. But she exuded love – real love. The producers, usually quite blasé about such things, felt it as I did.

And it was real. As she told of her early years – baby out of wedlock, no job, no money – it didn't come across as "poor me" at all but as a story where she became "lucky". I don't usually hug guests but I spontaneously made an exception in this case.

Some say that she was in Anne Murray's shadow but I don't see it that way. Take a look at and compare their Christmas albums which show Anne singing traditional songs very nicely; Rita did her own stuff, much of which she wrote and is, or should be, a collector's item.

No, Anne and Rita were different performers entirely and Nova Scotia and Canada have a great deal to be proud of both of them.

Oscar Peterson was a great pianist whose humility obviously came naturally.

In preparing for the interview I learned he was a fly-fisherman so I tied a couple of flies for him and presented them to him as I introduced him as one of Canada's great fisherman – which he got a kick out of. Whether or not my offerings worked I can't say.

I remember listening to Oscar playing C Jam Blues and The Honeydripper back when I was in High School in the 40s and he was a budding star.

I asked him how he saw himself as a great pianist up against the likes of Nat "King" Cole (who was a jazz all-star until he discovered singing) and Art Tatum.

He was modest but not shy.

He had great regard for Cole but he felt it a tragedy for Jazz when he went commercial. He simply said that he hoped he was in the same company as Tatum – which by all accounts he was and some experts say he was the best of them all.

I asked him about an album he did where he sang and sounded not unlike Cole. Why didn't he do more? He replied that he didn't want to go down the same path as Cole. He was a musician who taught piano at several universities where he was treated not as a jazz star but a skilled musician – which he was.

Peterson was Canadian and he laughingly told me how hard it was for Americans to accept that a great black musician could be Canadian. He had sincere praise for other musicians like Stan Getz with whom he did a great album – this was before iTunes made the terms "album" and "compact disc" terms of the past.

Oscar Peterson qualifies for the term "great" as a musician, as a Canadian and as a human being.

This will be the shortest of snapshots of guests.

I interviewed **Dizzy Gillespie**, one of the founders of "Bop" music. We conversed for half an hour and I didn't understand a word he said. Whether or not he understood me I don't know – what I can say is that he evidently spoke Bebop and I did not.

Seemed like a nice guy, I thought.

UNITED STATES

Jimmy Carter came to me for a very unusual reason – he had written a neat little book on fly-fishing. The ex-president had, in fairly recent days, been bitten by the fly-fishing bug and his experiences brought out the author in him. I don't remember much about the interview except when I disobeyed orders by asking him how he felt when the American hostages in Iran were released the day Ronald Reagan replaced him in the White House. Apparently Carter's people made his appearance on my show conditional on not being any political questions. I gave no such undertaking.

Instead of walking away from the question he gave a detailed and well thought out – and gracious answer.

I admire Jimmy Carter and think he was a better president than the generally Republican media portray him and I suspect that my audience came away from the interview thinking as I did, that we had listened to a class act.

I first met **Ralph Nader** at a private dinner in Victoria in 1976 before he was to take the stage for a lecture at the Royal Theatre. He was both fascinating and dull at the same time. Fascinating because he had done so much to change the automobile industry with his blockbuster book, **Unsafe At Any Speed**; dull because he tended to drone on, especially when he had the stage all to himself. I next met him in the run up to the 2004 US Presidential election in which he was determined to run. I asked him the questions you would expect about splitting the vote (which he did) but essentially got nowhere. In fact, he probably cost Al Gore the presidency and was responsible for inflicting George W. Bush on the world.

Back in the spring of 1947 I took my girlfriend, Heather, to see **Frankie Laine** at the Palomar Supper Club which was on the southwest corner of what is now the Burrard Building. Laine was all the rage and I remember he signed a street photograph of Heather and me saying "to Rafe and Heather, Thanks, Frankie Laine".

This was after a matinee which supper clubs usually ran, for kids, for a dollar each. That was a fair amount in an era where working people were happy to make a dollar an hour. But it was worth it.

About 20 years later, Eve and I went to the Cave Supper Club, with some friends, for dinner and entertainment by Frankie Laine. After the show I went up to his dressing room to get some autographs and said to Frankie, "I used to go to Seattle just so I could get your releases on the Atlas label which weren't available in Canada".

He was surprised and asked me what I had. I was able to string out about a dozen songs and Laine was amazed.

"What are you doing now?" he asked and when I told him that we were going home – it was well after midnight and midweek meaning I had to work.

Laine had other plans. He said to the effect that anyone who had gone out of his way to get the rare Atlas label deserved a vote of thanks and would my wife and I join him at a superb Italian restaurant across the street (I've forgotten the name) for dinner?

I went back to the table and told all that not only did I have Frankie Laine's autograph but that he was coming to the table and then taking us to dinner. Everyone was suitably impressed. Frankie came down, we said good night to our friends and went across the street for a delicious dinner suitably combined with Chianti. I don't remember much of the occasion but Frankie, having determined that I was truly a Frankie Laine fan, invited me to his room in the Georgia Hotel at 1:00 the following afternoon where he would play some of his latest writings – he did write songs but the only one that became, mildly, popular was "It Only Happens Once". Happily I had an easy day and I went and listened to his music and chatted with him for over an hour.

Fast-forward to 2002 and I interviewed Frankie Laine when he was well into his 80s. When I opened I said "you would never remember but my wife Eve and I had dinner with you after your performance at the Cave. Laine immediately said, "I was wondering where I remembered that name from – yes I remember you."

We had a great chat and though he might have been bs-ing me about remembering me it felt very good.

Laine had a sports incident of note. The Tournament of Champions, golf, used to have a Calcutta where people would "buy" a player and if he won, the successful bidder would get several hundreds of thousand dollars – when that was a hell of a lot of money. Three years in a row Laine bought Gene Littler who won all three times clearing about $1 million for Laine, considerably more than Littler – in those days the winner's share was $20,000.

Incidentally, Vancouver's Stan Leonard won this championship in 1958.

Frankie Laine - a great singer, a generous host and a super guest.

UNITED KINGDOM

The late **Anita Roddick** was the founder of The Body Shop. She was funny but serious. She hated capitalism and capitalists though she became one of the richest people in the world and tried to give the money away but made it too fast!

Though she sold out her main interest in the Body Shop she remained a director.

I found that Ms. Roddick oozed sex appeal and one of my producers later said she "was hitting on me" which was dubious in the extreme but flattered me no end.

Ms. Roddick's hatred of "the City", London's Wall Street, knew no bounds. She was passionate in her caring for animals and maintained that none of her products are tested first on animals though there are some who say otherwise.

A very interesting person indeed; her early death a tragedy.

Lord Montague of Beaulieu, (pronounced BE-WLY) is heir to not only one of the finest stately homes in Britain but also to the National Motor Museum, created by Lord Montague's father.

This museum has cars, cars, and more cars, plus hands-on exhibits, rides, a monorail, and gardens, driving games and parklands. The Palace House is built around the gatehouse of a Cistercian Abbey, which contains the usual tourist stop including an exhibition about the monks.

Like an oak from an acorn, the whole project first began in the Front Hall of Palace House, the family home when a mere five veteran vehicles were put on show. The place was opened to visitors in 1952, as a fitting tribute to Lord Montague's father who was well-known in his day for his enthusiastic support for early motoring. Since then, the collection has grown to over 300 vehicles of all types and added a vast selection of associated items. In fact, so large are the numbers now that, even with the huge exhibition hall, it's only possible to show around 250 vehicles at any one time.

But I knew there was more to this interview than met the eye – yet I didn't know what that entailed.

In 1954 Montague was imprisoned for twelve months for consensual homosexual offences along with journalist Peter Wildeblood and Michael Pitt-Rivers.

In my own defense, there was no Internet with "Google" and I'm not sure how I would have handled the information. What was of great interest is the Wolfenden Report and how it led to the removal of homosexuality as a crime and I wish I'd asked him how it felt to be singled out where Noel Coward, Somerset Maugham, John Gielgud and Cecil Beaton to name a few prominent gays were not.

In any event, I stuck with motor cars without dealing with the most interesting part of the story!

Prince Charles is a strange man as we all know from what we hear but all I can say after meeting him twice, once at Government House in Victoria and the other at his home at Highgrove in Gloucestershire, is that he is a grand master of spouting the inane crap such people are known for and bred to use.

The only other thing I noticed was that he is always playing with his cuff links.

He sort of reminds me of Prince George of Denmark, married to Queen Anne, whose uncle, Charles II once said of him "I've tried him drunk and I've tried him sober and there's nothing in him."

The foregoing was, of course, unfair. The social march senior royals must do for their lifetime is inhuman.

My second meeting was at a sort of field house on his estate at Highgrove and I was amongst perhaps 30 journalists from all over the world.

Charles no doubt has had a lot of very bad press while in fact he is owed a debt of considerable proportion for the charity work he's done and for protecting Paternoster Square by St. Paul's from the ravages of developers and their architects.

I still wonder if it wouldn't be better to have buttoned cuffs although I suppose that there are worse habits than playing with your cuff links.

Prince Andrew is quite a different breed of a cat from his older brother. I met him at another reception at Government House in Victoria. I actually managed to have a decent talk with His Royal Highness about fishing.

"Fergie", his former wife, had made headlines and I would have loved to chat a bit about toe sucking but thought better of it.

SWEETHEART OF THE ARMED FORCES

During World War II the Entertainment sector was hard at work performing for the boys and girls at war. One of the very best was Vera Lynn who was called the Sweetheart Of The Armed Forces. Many of her songs were hits. I think of *There'll Always be an England, There'll Be Bluebirds Over the White Cliffs of Dover, When the Lights Go On Again All Over The World* and, of course, *We'll Meet Again*.

I first saw Dame Vera in London on May 8, 1995 - a celebration of the 50th anniversary of the end of the war in Europe - at a gala concert in Hyde Park, London, held in a large temporary outdoor concert hall at Speaker's Corner. There were TV monitors throughout the park bringing the total to about 250,000 people according to the police. The theme was London musicals over the years, interspersed with appearances by famous people including the Queen. Dame Vera sang three times.

We were seated beside a group who were all East Enders with food baskets and wine. The East End of London had taken an awful pasting during the war and the group had a marvelous time singing along *Knees Up Mother Brown* and the like.

When Robert Hardy (of All Creatures Great and Small) came on to give Churchill's speech on VE Day you could hear a pin drop. "Never in our long history have we seen a day like this one," Hardy intoned... Then one of the ladies next to us rose and shouted "and we stood alone". It was an awesome moment raising the hackles and filling the eyes...

Vera closed the show with *We'll Meet Again* accompanied by 250,000 throats and half a million teary eyes singing along. It was truly a time to remember.

In 1995, I believe it was, Dame Vera Lynn came to Vancouver to help veterans remember the wars.

She was a charming guest. During the last break just before the time was up, we closed with the great war song, her signature tune, *We'll Meet Again,* and I got to sing along – off air of course – with Dame Vera Lynn, a very great woman who so inspired the armed forces and the general public when inspiration was badly needed.

Interviewing **J.K. Rowley** of Harry Potter

books was a cloak and dagger affair. It wasn't until a few minutes before the show that I learned that a studio had been constructed for the purpose in the Waterfront Hotel so Ms. Rowling could avoid the press and the public. Remember, this was at the height of her fame. She was a very nice person and modest if not a tad shy.

One of my more interesting guests, whom I interviewed both at his flat overlooking the Houses of Parliament, and my studio, was **Jeffrey Archer, now Lord Archer of Weston-Super-Mare.** Of course I interviewed him about his books but mostly we talked about politics – from the Tory side of course.

For my first interview I interviewed him three times in one day. After #1, when I got to my train I decided to listen to it. Not there. I had somehow erased it.

I phoned his secretary and she graciously arranged another interview. It was one of those days, for when I again hit Charing Cross Station I found I had done it again!

Back I went and Archer had a high old time giving me the gears but I got the interview and it was there!

I interviewed him probably 10 times in all including at least two in my Vancouver studio.

He was the quintessential insider and fascinating no less so for being sent to jail for perjury, as well he should have been. But like everyone, he had a redeeming feature – he was generous.

After one interview with him in his flat high above the Thames, Wendy and I walked over to St Margaret's Church near Westminster Abbey when she discovered that her purse had been stolen. Thieves in Europe are masters at this as my former wife Patti found in Paris where the same thing happened.

We thought about this and remembered that she had been jostled while crossing the Vauxhall Bridge. Hoping against hope that she'd left the purse at Lord Archer's, we went back but it wasn't there. The principal problem was the loss of passports and travellers cheques (this was still a time when most smaller stores and eating establishments didn't take credit cards).

Archer asked if we had any money and since we'd lost the Travellers Cheques we would have nothing until we got to the Amex office. Archer peeled off two fifties and handed them to me, then instructed his driver to take us to the police station in his Daimler to report the theft, then to Amex at Charing Cross for travellers cheques, and finally to the High Commission office to deal with the lost passports.

There is good in everyone.

CHURCHILLIANS

I do show my prejudices in having a special category for my hero, **Sir Winston Churchill**.

I am a Churchillian. I listened to the great man

with my parents during the Second World War. I collect his books, am a member of the Churchill Society and lap up their quarterly magazine Finest Hour. I should add that to be a Churchillian is not to be blind to his faults and mistakes; to do that is to trivialize the man who unquestionably was the greatest man of the 20th century. Of course I never met let alone interviewed Churchill but I was lucky enough to interview several around him.

I start with **Sir Martin Gilbert,** his biographer (8 volumes of about 1000 pages per volume), because he is still very active.

Sir Martin Gilbert is probably the most productive top-notch historian of all time with, at this writing, more than 75 books to his credit. And unlike the stuff I put out, his are all deeply researched, and serious. He took over Churchill's Official Biography after Churchill's son, Randolph Churchill, died with two volumes completed leaving Sir Martin to do the last six. Any who have read all eight – and I certainly have – must marvel at the detail, especially in the last six books, plus his assembly of ten huge companion volumes of Churchill's documents. Incidentally, Sir Martin denies being the "Official" biographer because, as he has said, that description is somewhat misleading. As he said in an interview with Brian Lamb on C-Span's Book-notes in 1991:

"I'm called the official biographer, though to the enormous credit of the Churchill family they've never asked to see a single word of what I was writing until the books were printed and bound and ready for sale to the public. They never asked me to delete a word or to skirt around a particular issue. So 'official' is a misnomer if it's thought to mean a censored or restricted biographer."

I would say that his biography of the great Churchill is the achievement of 100 lifetimes but he has, amongst many, many other first class books, as his website notes, done the definitive history of the Holocaust. His book **The Holocaust: The Jewish Tragedy** (published in the United States as **The Holocaust: A History of the Jews of Europe During the Second World War**) is a classic work on the subject. Indeed, at this writing I'm reading a book of letters to a Jewish lady in India that outlines the history of Jews back to Adam and Eve.

I have found Sir Martin to be concise and rather humourless to interview but I suppose after a writer of his attainments gets the same questions about Churchill thrown at him ad nauseum it's hard to be funny. Through the gravitas, the interviewer detects a man with the same capacity for work as his famous subject with, dare I say it, more thorough research. Mind you, Sir Martin has not been called upon to run too many wars!

If nothing else, one should "Google" Sir Martin's bibliography and you will, like all who read it, be staggered by the output of this man who is not yet 70.

I must also mention a book of Churchill's words called **Churchill: The Power of Words**, which I heartily endorse not so much for the history but as a living example of the beauty of the English language whether written or spoken.

Sir William Deakin was a history professor at Oxford who would come to Chartwell from Oxford every Saturday to help Churchill with his **History Of The English Speaking Peoples**. A charming man, he told me of the time he phoned Churchill on a Friday to say he couldn't make it that weekend.

"That's fine, Bill, we'll meet you at the station", Churchill replied. "But," said Deakin, "I cannot make it." To which the great man responded "that's just fine, we'll meet you at the station as usual."

And, as Deakin told me, he was at Chartwell at the usual time and place.

Grace Hamblin was Churchill's lead secretary to whom Churchill dictated often right through the night. The secretaries could not take his words in shorthand but had to type them as they came. He could be foul tempered if things didn't work to his satisfaction.

"Why did you put up with this?" I asked.

"Because he was a very great man and we loved him," was the reply.

Anthony Montague Browne was Churchill's principal secretary from 1952 until Churchill's death in 1965. He wrote a book on the subject called **The Long Sunset,** a marvelous insight into how Churchill coped with advancing years, unhappily for the most part. The book is a great read.

Winston Churchill II was Winston's grandson and a MP in the eighties and nineties. Following in the footsteps of his father and grandfather he was a good journalist. He wrote a book, not of much interest to me at any rate, but I interviewed him in his office in the House of Commons.

In 1995 an extraordinary thing happened. It was the 50th anniversary of VE day, the end of the war in Europe. My former law partner and long-time friend, Stanley Winfield, Wendy and I had just been at a celebration at Buckingham Palace and were walking down Buckingham Palace Road searching for a pub. Stan, who had been in London on VE day, was wearing his medals. Suddenly, out of this immense crowd came a man with two teenage boys.

He said to Stan, "I see from your medals you're a Canadian ... I'm Winston Churchill and these are my boys Randolph and Jack." We chatted for a bit and it was a surreal feeling. I, of course, said that I had interviewed him not all that long ago and he politely pretended that he remembered.

The best for the last.

Mary, Lady Soames. Churchill had 5 children, one, Marigold died in early childhood. The youngest of these was Mary, now Lady Soames, born in 1922 and at this writing still going strong. During the war Mary was very much in harm's way working in an anti-aircraft post in Hyde Park.

She married one of Churchill's junior ministers, Christopher Soames, who became famous for settling the Rhodesia dispute in 1978 for which he received a life peerage.

I was privileged to interview Lady Soames, on three occasions and what a marvellous, and may I say, beautiful lady she is. Her's were those kinds of interviews you didn't want to end.

Lady Soames is also an author and I would highly recommend all three books- **Clementine Churchill: The Biography of a Marriage - Winston and Clementine, A Daughter's Tale, and The Memoir of Winston Churchill's Youngest Child.**

CHAPTER EIGHT

People, Programs and Chauncey

SPECIAL PROGRAMS

Special programs formed a big part of my career in radio.

The obvious ones would be psychics and astrologers and I did several over the years. The problem is that they have a "tune-out" as well as a "tune-in" effect. If you're looking for an easy hour with lots of phone calls there's nothing like them. But I had long ago discovered that the full phone board did not necessarily demonstrate that the audience was large, only that there is a lot of people who believe in that sort of stuff.

For a few years I had psychics Kristofir and Krystal (I think I remember how they spell their names!) who had a large following. They jammed the phone lines but I began to feel uneasy.

I began to worry about some of the serious business advice they were giving, and felt that unless I was confident that they knew what they were talking about (I wasn't) I was exposing myself and CKNW to trouble, even law suits. Quite apart from that, I was letting my listeners be possibly misled. My confidence faltered badly when I asked them about a business event (whether I was going to be offered a certain job) and they were wrong.

In any event, I dropped psychics, astrologers and the like.

One of my favourite regulars was Santa in the form of the late Bob Dawson whom we met earlier in the CJOR tale. He was a very talented broadcaster in his own right and he brought that in spades to the show.

Bob was always prepared. He would check out all the toys that were fashionable at the time so when the timid little voice mentioned a toy that I at any rate hadn't heard of, he knew all about it. He also knew how to make kids and adults laugh at the same joke but for different reasons.

He added a new character to the Christmas gang in Olive, Rudolph's girlfriend ("all of" the other reindeer!). Bob would get the kids to sing Jingle Bells and it was great fun to hear these little monotones do the "hey" part.

We had one marvellous session when a little girl from Trail had lost her little dog "Sparky" and wanted Santa to do something about it. This was tough because the child had such faith. Santa could do little.

As I was doing the extro to the Noon news and the end of the show, I got a frantic wave from Shiral in the control room – Sparky had been found! We went overtime and the little girl and her Mom effused their gratitude.

It was hard to keep a dry eye.

I loved doing **Law Day**.

The B.C. Law Society had an annual "Law Week" and we started doing a very different show. It began with David Lloyd George Elementary who put Hansel and Gretel on trial – all credit to the teachers who thought of this idea. I'm delighted that they did!

The kids came all dressed up in the appropriate costumes. One was Hansel, another Gretel, one the witch and there was a prosecutor and so on. I was the judge and the audience was the jury.

As judge, I summed up very opposed to the defendants and the audience played along as jurors and smote the unfair judge and acquitted the accused.

We did several kangaroo courts – The Trial of Peter Rabbit was a favourite. As judge, of course, I took Mr. MacGregor's side. The jury found for Peter, needless to say. What fun it all was and I felt like a cheater taking the station's money for this pleasure.

One of my long-standing regular shows was

the annual visit of **Peter Luongo** and the **Langley Ukulele Ensemble**. Peter had started this band and taken it to winning roles in Hawaii and waypoints. One of the lads, James Hill, is now a world-renowned virtuoso. It was great fun bantering with the kids and to see new ones each year, often the brother or sister of a past player. I loved the ukulele and so, evidently, did the listeners.

I don't know how it came about but I started a couple of series with Professor **Paul Budra** of Simon Fraser University. Paul is Associate Dean of English and amongst several things is an expert on Shakespeare.

I was very taken with this idea because, like all kids, I had studied a couple of Shakespeare plays and had always wanted to continue to do this as an adult but never quite got around to it. Part of this was fear I'd get messed up by the language. I had seen some plays and films but secretly wanted more.

Paul was truly amazing. He brought the characters to life, and for very good reason he became very popular indeed.

Paul also did a series for us on "thrillers" which was hugely popular.

Speaking of Shakespeare, **Christopher Gaze**, originator and manager of the **Bard on the Beach,** would do a show with us to open the season. Christopher, in addition to his many gifts, is a wonderful actor and no show was complete without him doing his rousing version of Henry V's speech at Agincourt. He did this at a 2011 "roast" in honour of my 80th and he brought the house down.

The Bard on the Beach has become a hugely valuable addition to our city. Wendy and I are members and regulars.

One of my favourite shows I did every Friday with my very talented friend, **Shiral Tobin**, called the **Under 40s Club**. We talked about everything and took calls on any subject from younger adults. Shiral was indeed under 40 and I, of course, was only 39 – or so.

One day I took a caller (male) who wanted an opinion from Shiral on oral sex, was it good or bad? Uncertain what to do but thinking I should quickly take another call, I was staggered to hear Shiral give a very complete summary – in favour!

I expected an onslaught from irate listeners but not a peep! Shiral could (pardon the expression) pull it off! That she hasn't got her own major show is a great mystery.

It was great fun.

In 2002, I think it was, we did a political show with former NDP MLA **David Schreck** and whomever we could get to stand up to him. For quite a while we had trouble getting the right person – all males and all unable to deal with David - and eventually settled on **Erin Airton** (now Chutter). She could handle David, and then some on occasion.

In my opinion it was the best political program I ever did. Both were brilliant and while each had their Party, neither were elected thus had no formal allegiance to contend with. After my days at CKNW we reconvened on AM600.

Kathy Ruddick, a world-class fly-fisher owned, with her husband Malcolm, **Ruddick's Fly Shop**, and during the season did a short stint on Fridays on what was happening in lakes around the province, what insects were hatching and what fly patterns were most suitable.

Kathy's sunny personality and solid knowledge were plain to all listeners. You wouldn't think that fly-fishing would be a hot topic but I can't begin to tell you how many people would tell me, "I don't even fish but I wouldn't miss Kathy for anything."

People also like pets and I was able to satisfy that with a vet, **Dr Moe Milstein** and a dog trainer, **Ann Jackson**.

Dr Moe has a very broad knowledge, a large practice called Blue Cove Animal Hospital in North Vancouver near the North Shore end of the Ironworkers Bridge, and a beautiful laid back sense of humour. He has been vet for the Mair family for over 30 years.

Ann, whose black lab Dana is a sister to our late chocolate lab Chauncey, is wonderful at giving solutions for various habits our dogs pick up. We've been pals with Ann for 25 years. When, 12 years ago, we lost our chocolate lab Clancy, I asked Ann to find me a good breeder and she sent me to

Big Valley Labradors. I phoned Agneta and Willy and this begat a fascinating email exchange as Agneta wanted to know that one of her pups was going to a good home and I wanted to make sure my dog to be was not too closely inbred. Wendy has kept this fun exchange.

They had a black bitch that had been bred to Rascal, a chocolate which, though not guaranteed, should mean some chocolate puppies. I took first dibs on a chocolate male. While we were in London that fall I got a fax from Ann saying, "Congratulations you're a father!"

Turned out that there were 8 puppies that lived, only two chocolates, one male and he was chocolate. A few days later we went out to Agneta and Willy's place with Ann who, very shortly after we got there, said, "I knew I shouldn't have come a few days ago because Labrador litters are impossible to resist and I just bought a female!" We had several offers to sell our right to Chauncey but there was no chance of that – Big Valley's Chauncey of Deveron was ours! And whenever I write or speak about him, as now, I weep.

We have a hot tub and every Wednesday for over 11 years a wonderful guy named Jack Bilodeau cleans the pool for us. He is a dog lover and breeder and Chauncey and he became great pals. Jack would take Chauncey when we were away and eventually he would take him when Wendy was visiting her daughter and granddaughter in Winnipeg.

Early in 2013, Chauncey developed a chronic larynx problem and we knew it would take him in the not too distant future. He now tired easily but as it is with labs, he refused to slow down.

In August 2013 Jack had Chauncey and with one of his dogs, had gone to Ambleside in West Vancouver and Chauncey immediately went swimming as he would when we walked him. It was just for a moment but as we all knew, one day he wouldn't be able to breathe any more. And it happened. And Jack took him to the Vet and we both blubbered as we learned he wasn't going to make it. I can't drive any more so it was impossible for me to make it from Lions Bay to Blue Ridge Mountain Animal Hospital and Chauncey died in the arms of the person that, next to Wendy, he loved more than anyone in the world – a love reciprocated by Jack.

After it was over, Jack came over and though I hadn't had a drink of hard liquor since my 50th birthday, I poured each of us a triple Irish Whiskey from Wendy's supply. We cried like children with Jack blaming himself for something that was bound to happen to someone who even took Chauncey for a walk. With Labs, the innate desire to run, retrieve and swim forever challenges the ability to do so.

We and Jack have become great friends.

A little humour. When Jack first took Chauncey he took him on his rounds – until Chauncey without a by-your-leave jumped into the pool Jack was servicing for a little dip. The owner was not impressed. Thereafter, Chauncey stayed in the truck with Jack's dogs!

Every tax time and usually three other times of the year we had Chartered Accountant **Russ Wilson** on the show to talk taxes and other accountant stuff for small businesses and individual taxpayers. Russ – and this is so typical – in order to make himself a better guest, took a course in broadcasting at the BC Institute Of Technology.

In one lesson two broadcasting pieces were played. After my example, the teacher said, "That's not what you want to be," and after the other with Peter Gzowski said, "That's the proper way."

According to Russ, a fellow student raised his hand and asked, "If Gzowski is the right way and Rafe is the wrong way, how come Rafe has all the listeners?"

Russ was, with very good reason, very popular. He was down to earth and, unlike other professionals, spoke the language of the people not the balance sheet.

MY LOVE AFFAIR WITH BRIAN BURKE

One Thanksgiving we had asked Brian Burke, an executive with the Vancouver Canucks, to come on the show and give my listeners the skinny on the season that had just started.

He agreed, then at the last moment cancelled because, he said, "Rafe has said some things disloyal to the Canucks!" Apparently it's OK to be disloyal to your premier or prime minister but not the Canucks.

I was pissed off because Thanksgiving is hard to program and we had already promoted Burke's appearance. As they say, however, what goes around comes around, and some months later Burke made a big commotion about scalpers selling tickets at the Coliseum where the Canucks played in those days.

I commented at the top of my show, "Where the hell does Burke think they get those tickets and whatever happened to free enterprise? Obviously from the Canucks and when a game is not well attended, the Canucks are very grateful to the scalpers having bought their tickets."

I went on in these words – "Brian Burke is a first class asshole and he gets into the asshole hall of fame without the customary waiting period – and right now he's on the phone to CKNW trying to get me fired!"

I forgot all about it. When I got off air Fin called me and said, "Rafe, you're in trouble."

I asked why and he replied, "Because of the remarks made about Brian Burke ... Doug Rutherford (the program director) called me and said they're going to suspend you."

I said, "Fin, under our contract there is no provision for suspending me ... they have to fire me and that means a full year's pay plus COLA, thanks to that neat contract you got for me!"

"Hadn't you best phone Doug?"

"To hell with him."

Within a minute Doug was on the line saying, "I'm coming over to your house, leaving right now."

I replied, "You're not welcome in my home."

We agreed to meet in the boardroom at the Expo site studio with Fin being there as well.

Before going any further let me say I love Doug - he was a hell of a good program manager and was and remains a good friend. His job was a tough one. You have to understand that we weren't doing some sort of nicely, nicely talk show but a program that held to the hot flames the tootsies of all in authority. No punches were pulled. No prisoners taken.

Doug arrived black with anger. Clearly he was under orders to get me to apologize or else. "Do you know what the Vancouver Canucks mean to CKNW?"

"Of course, Doug. Mr. Griffiths owns them both."

"No ... do you know anything of the financial affairs?"

"Of course. CKNW makes a lot of money broadcasting their games. Does that mean we suspend free speech when dealing with them."

(I should add that I was by far not the only CKNW broadcaster who had badmouthed the Canucks. Al Davidson had been banned from their dressing room and both Neil Macrae and Frosty Forst had had heat applied to them.)

Doug then went to the meat of the matter.

"This isn't about free speech ... I want you to apologize to Burke tomorrow morning."

"Doug," I said, "You look good and healthy: if you live to a hundred that's not going to happen."

Doug stormed out, tears of anger in his eyes.

There is an interesting sequel.

A few weeks later Doug was promoted to General Manager of WIC's station in Edmonton, CHED, and there was a bit of a going away ceremony for him at Me 'n Ed's Pizza.

Ted Smith, President of WIC radio stations, made a speech about Doug and said, "As I told him when he was promoted, at least you won't have to deal with Rafe any more." He went on to say, "Doug came into my office a couple of weeks ago demanding that we get him a new briefcase. He showed me his and it had a big hole – obviously punched in – and Doug said, 'I've just come from a meeting with Rafe.'"

It was the Burke meeting.

This is the right place, I think, to talk about Ted Smith. He was the manager of CKNW when I arrived and president of the radio stations thereafter until Corus bought them out. I always thought that Ted didn't like me very much so, accordingly, I didn't like him very much. I was wrong, very wrong. I learned later that he was my backstop at the station and that to get me fired meant getting Ted to agree, which was highly unlikely. In the early 90s WIC, through Ted, paid my entry fee to the Royal Vancouver Yacht Club and arranged my election to it. As time went on I learned what a friend I really had in Ted and I hope he reads this.

Before I go on, let me explain that my philosophy towards the station was schizophrenic, in the dictionary not medical sense. On the one hand I loved the station and was proud of it, at least until Corus' corrosive fingers got onto the levers. I was immensely proud of my own performance and if that seems egotistical why shouldn't I be proud? I started with them as a broke man in his fifties who had, it seemed, failed in radio … and they, especially Ted Smith, had confidence in me and stuck with me through both good and bad.

On the other hand, I had to assert total independence. Sometimes that was unpleasant. But you have to do it as any good talk show host will affirm.

The good times vastly outnumbered the bad ones.

CKNW AND MENTAL ILLNESS

In the late 80s I decided that I had cancer of the liver and was going to die. The evidence was all there and I checked my symptoms with my Columbia Medical Dictionary and confirmed my self-diagnosis. I called my doctor's office and told the receptionist that I had to see the doctor immediately and, when she asked why, I told her it was because I had cancer of the liver.

There was a long pause and she told me I would have to wait until the next morning.

In my soft and gentle voice I said, "To hell with that. Goddamn it, I'm coming right over!"

It was late afternoon so I simply sat in the reception room. When the doctor emerged he came over and said, "Rafe, what's all this crap about liver cancer?"

I said, "Mel, I have it".

He examined me and, in his usual professional voice said, "Dammit, you idiot ... you don't have cancer of the liver, you have gall stones!"

I protested more vigorously so he agreed to get me to ultrasound.

I took that test which involves a technician running something that looks like a microphone over the target area and this casts an image on a screen. Every time she went over the liver area she frowned.

"It's cancer, isn't it?" I said.

She made no comment but summoned a doctor who likewise frowned at the magic spot.

"Tell me, doctor, I can take it" (I couldn't.) "It's cancer isn't it?"

He asked me to turn on my side then gave me a rabbit punch just under the rib cage on the right side. "Did that hurt?"

"Not really although I wouldn't want you to do it all day long."

He punched me again, looked up at the screen then said, "That's done it – you had a gallstone stuck in the entrance to the gall bladder. That was your problem."

"You mean that after all that I just needed my chiropractor?!"

The next day I saw Mel again and he retold me the good news to which I replied, "You're all lying to me."

"How long ago was it that your daughter was killed?" Mel asked.

"What the hell has that got to do with liver cancer?"

"Rafe, I'm going to ask you some questions which may seem silly but please answer them."

At question 3 I started to sob uncontrollably, and Mel held on to me as if I were a child until I stopped bawling.

"Rafe, you have depression, which in your case manifests itself in what are commonly called panic attacks. This anxiety isn't a character flaw - the attacks are very real and there is nothing you, yourself, can do about them. This is caused by a shortness of what is known as serotonin in the brain and it is the same sort of problem you have in your pancreas with insulin. You have no more reason to be ashamed of mental illness than you are of diabetes. We'll now start looking for medicine for you."

We did that and lucked out with Elavil. Within a few weeks I hadn't felt so good for years.

I told no one except my *then* wife, Patti, whose attitude was not unusual … "Well, you have your drugs and I'll have my wine." Not terribly helpful.

Some years later I was interviewing a hotshot psychiatrist from the US and in the station breaks we discussed my case. After hearing that I took Elavil he said, "That's the tin lizzie of medicines – you should be on Serzone."

I saw Mel and told him I wanted to switch to Serzone, to which he replied "You dumb bugger … if it ain't broke, don't fix it!"

But I persisted so he gave me a prescription and warned me that I had to be off all meds for two weeks. It happened that my *now* wife Wendy and I were off to London and Paris for a couple of weeks so there would be no pressure, thus no problem. Right?

Wrong. On our first day in London we took a long walk from our hotel to Covent Garden. It was a warm pleasant day but I was shivering so much I went into a Tie Rack and bought a scarf. By the time we reached our destination, I was shivering even more so I bought a wool sweater.

When we got back to our hotel, called Jurys (now the Kensington), I was soaked in sweat, shaking like a leaf and I started crying. For the whole trip, Wendy did everything she could do to help but it was not a great vacation, that's for sure.

When I got back home, I confessed my errors to Mel and got back on Elavil post haste!

My doctor knew about depression and what to do. He took the time and made the effort to attend seminars on depression. I dare say 80% of family doctors hadn't a clue. To Doctor Melvin Bruchet

– now retired - I owe a great deal, perhaps even my life.

But I was lucky not only to have Mel as my doctor but also to find the right medicine.

I started to do radio shows on the subject in an attempt to help people overcome the huge stigma attached to mental illness. On many shows my guest was a family doctor from New Westminster, Dr. Teresa Hogarth, most of whose practice was with the mentally ill. Because mental illness takes much more time than an ordinary doctor's visit, for which the MSP won't pay, Dr. Hogarth simply couldn't make a living and had to go to work for a pharmaceutical company. This is an elementary example of how the mentally ill are discriminated against. Teresa was a terrific spokesperson and practitioner yet couldn't afford to help mentally ill people.

One call I took – this would have been around 1992 – really got to me. A middle-aged man related a story so much like my own that I heard myself saying, "Sir, you sound just like me a few years ago. To hell with what your wife says - see a doctor."

One part of me couldn't believe what I was saying. I had "come out" so to speak, although that wasn't my intention. It should have been and I don't regret it for a moment.

I talked it over with CKNW management and the manager said, "Anything we can do, just tell us - we'll help."

I decided to help the BC Branch of the Canadian Mental Health Association with their annual "Depression Screening" day, by putting a bank of a dozen phones, off-air; while on-air I would promote this and also take calls to Dr. Hogarth. In the sense that hundreds called in it was a resounding success but the nagging fear was that they weren't getting help because so little was available.

In frustration I met Bev Guttray, the managing director of BC Branch of the CMHA, and suggested we could, with the support of unions and management, help mentally ill employees. We set up the annual Bottom Line Conference, which brings together management, unions, professionals – indeed all who can help. Last year was their 10th anniversary.

There is so much more to tell but this is about my radio years not causes. Let me close with a bad news, good news bit.

The bad news is that my long association with the BC Branch of the Canadian Mental Health Association (of which I was Patron) ended nastily. It happened thusly:

Since the late Nancy Hall had, effectively, been fired as the people's Mental Health Advocate and the Liberals weren't about to replace her, I decided that it might be a good idea if I were to become a private mental health advocate and go around the province making people aware of mental illness, by talking to the media, service clubs, doctors, church groups and so on. I asked Bev Guttray, the Executive Director of the BC Branch of CMHA to help me, not with money, but their contacts around the province. Pretty small favour but after several weeks of hemming and hawing she refused on the basis I was seen as too *political.*

Now I wasn't too political to speak at countless meetings for them, do videos for them and start the Bottom Line Conference; nor was I too political to receive several awards from the CMHA including The National Award to broadcasters.

I left the BC Branch, CMHA, and resigned as patron. My resignation was greeted with acceptance in indecent haste.

The man who pays the piper calls the tune and Bev buckled under to pressure from the provincial government, to whom I have never bent the knee, as Bev obviously felt she had to do or suffer financially.

A last word about CKNW.

Not only did CKNW support what I was doing by encouragement and tangible ways, they have given assistance and understanding to their ‚broadcasters and staff and they have been leaders in industry on this issue. I'm proud of them.

CHAPTER NINE
End of Daze

My on-air career ended in October 2005 when I was fired from 600AM. It came on the heels of the manager Gerry Siemens complaining that I was, according to his golfing partners, talking too much about fish farms.

I replied, "Why don't you ask your fishing friends?"

Interestingly, a few weeks before I was canned, in a write-in ballot to The Georgia Straight, I was declared #1 broadcaster in my field.

This leave-taking left bad taste with me for both for Siemens and Pattison, as they cheated me out of $3500. I was on a three-year contract with a COLA clause for each of those years. Siemens canned me with 10 months to go, paid me for that last year as he was obliged to, but refused to pay the COLA. It came to about $7000 and after I threatened to sue Siemens he offered me half. I had no inkling to spend hours fighting in Small Claims Court so I took it.

I take comfort in the aphorism "what goes around comes around".

I LEAVE CKNW – INVOLUNTARILY

To this day I don't know why I was fired in June of 2003. I must be careful to note that what the station did is terminate the contract that provided my services to CKNW.

One of the terms of my firing was that they would only pay me out if I agreed not to give the reasons. You'll note that it was they, not I, who didn't want the public to know the truth. They had no right to do this. Under the contract, if they wanted to terminate me, they had to pay me – period. But I knew that if I didn't agree they would deny liability then bit-by-bit make offers, causing me legal fees and much anguish. In short, I signed under duress. Moreover, the story was already out with my press release two days before so I regard that stipulation a just a bit of Corus nastiness. If the object was to keep the lady's name out of things, as I mentioned I never have and I regard her as just an excuse for Corus to get rid of me. Indeed, I haven't even mentioned the manager's name...

Here is the amazing story.

I had, less than six months before, signed a new contract which contained a substantial raise. Until April 2003 I received no complaint from people who worked for me. One day in April 2003 the manager took me to lunch at the Four Seasons

Hotel – not in a restaurant but in a small meeting room in the middle of which was a small table with a tray of sandwiches by each chair.

Over the table – I'm not making this up – there was a light. We sat down and the manager started asking me questions from a large note pad. He alleged that I had harassed my producer by such things as forcing her to bring me coffee, forcing her to come to coffee with me, forcing her to put sprinkles on my coffee at Starbucks, using the "'f" word (one of the commonest words in the radio business) and matters of that sort. No, there was no suggestion of any sexual harassment, and there was none. What astonished me was that my relationship with the lady had been excellent until this – I had paid her a $500 bonus out of my own for two straight Christmases and loaned her my car when I was away.

On a regular basis from then until I was fired the manager would come to my office, often just before I was going on air, to hassle me asking what I was going to do about these "heinous" crimes. On the last day I worked he did this and I told him to fuck off and "stay fucked off".

By way of aside not only would I never name the lady, when I was fired I sent her a note telling her that there were no hard feelings. It's a tough job producing a show like mine and perhaps the pressure was too much.

Two days before I was fired, a Vancouver Sun reporter called me and said he wanted to talk to me about "my sexual harassment" of my producer. I made it very clear that if anyone suggested such a thing I would instantly sue. I promised, however – since a story of my imminent firing was unfolding in the media – to issue a press release the next day telling what had happened, which I did in detail. When I was fired and the condition of silence was imposed, the entire local media already had my story, a story not in any way denied by CKNW.

Perhaps Christie Blatchford then of the Globe and Mail covered it all best in a column when she said that the station should have told her to "blow it out her ass".

The day I was fired on air, at the start of what was my show, was to say the least, hectic.

Brian Coxford of Global/BCTV asked to interview me at my home at one o'clock that afternoon and stupidly I refused, saying that my friend Russ Fraser (former BC Cabinet minister and a longtime friend) and I went sailing every Monday and I saw no reason to change that habit. I shouldn't have been surprised if Brian had gone on air and said I refused to be interviewed. Lucky for me that's not the way Brian is.

Then he asked if he could come down to the marina with a camera and I said, "Of course".

Brian filmed as my sailboat, *Somerled*, with Russ, Wendy, chocolate lab Chauncey and I cheerfully waving and smiling (except Chauncey who just wagged his tail) chugged out to open waters.

The story ran on the 6 o'clock BCTV/Global Evening News, off the top, for 13 minutes and the next but last shot showed the sailboat scene with our smiling waves while the last scene was of the CKNW brass putting their hands over the camera and refusing an interview.

I couldn't have bought better coverage than that!

By the next day, Wendy and I were worn out by calls from every direction so we decided to go to London for a week.

Upon my return there were two interesting messages.

One was from Gerry Siemens of 600AM who wanted me to come work with them.

The other was from Jack Webster Jr. who told me that I was the unanimous choice of the Awards Committee to be the recipient of The Bruce Hutchison Lifetime Achievement Award at the annual Jack Webster Dinner that fall. As I listened, I wept. Wendy and I had gone through a hell of a lot of angst and the Hutchison Award showed that my colleagues in the media had supported me even though I had been less than kind to many of them. This also demonstrated that I had always tried to help women get ahead.

The dinner that November had over 1000 guests, including my two daughters and a grandson with his lovely date.

Was or am I bitter? The plain answer is no – hurt, yes but in the radio business it's like wartime on the front – you can be killed anytime. I certainly had only the fondest memories of CKNW when Mr. Griffiths ran it. But I was very badly treated at the end by 'NW, after 19 years of consistent performance. Throughout my media days, I always knew I was on the edge of dismissal and several times I felt very close to it. But this way was simply unfair, especially since at no time did Corus complain about my performance. How the hell could they with the "numbers" I was getting?

I have since been told that it was Shaw Cable, the largest shareholder in Corus and controlled by a woman who was very concerned about women's rights, who demanded that I be punished. The key point was, evidently, that she wanted me to see the Human Resources department. I, frankly, don't believe this.

I don't think I would ever have dignified this foolishness by grovelling in this manner, but to have done so would have been illegal. As the manager who was harassing the hell out of me could apparently never understand, I was not a CKNW employee but an independent contractor and this wasn't just a silly little legal nit. The tax department looks very carefully at companies like mine because if I was only incorporated to avoid tax they would go beyond that and treat me as a CKNW employee. My company had in fact been born when I was not in radio but mostly doing writing, speaking and consulting on many issues. For me to submit to CKNW demands would tell the taxman that I was really an employee and it would have very serious consequences.

While a very substantial portion of the company's revenue came from outside radio and I have no doubt that on analysis the tax department would have agreed with me, I was not prepared to invite an audit. The Corus manager was a Chartered Accountant and should have understood this. (Interestingly, before he became General Manager for CKNW he managed a Meat plant. On one of our little meetings I told him that Stevie Cameron would like to blacken his eyes; he replied that would not be very *gentlemanly of him!* The manager of one of Canada's top radio stations didn't know that Stevie Cameron was a woman!)

No - bitterness is not the word. I was hurt to have been fired as I was. Had Corus, the new owners, wanted me to retire, at nearly 72 I would have done so as long as I was paid what was owed me and not restrained from working elsewhere.

I have been airbrushed out of CKNW's history. One of the conditions imposed on me was that I could never go to the 20th or 21st floor of the TD building without written permission from the manager. Can you believe it?

In September 2012 I went to the 20th floor, the reception area, and delivered a package for Simi Sara whom I consider to be a very good broadcaster. I've always tried to support women in the industry and this package was Sir Martin Gilbert's collection of Churchilliana called **The Power of**

Words. It took until mid-January 2013 for them to give Simi the book! I wrote the Program Director, Tom Plasteras (recently fired by NW) and accused them of petty childishness, to which I received no reply let alone explanation.

CKNW is losing in the ratings to CBC, for God's sake! I have not mentioned the Mother Corp until now because we would have committed mass hari kari if CBC had ever even been a factor.

Let me tell you a bit about the national broadcaster.

It's accepted amongst the chattering classes that the CBC – mostly because it allows no advertising – is the linchpin that holds the country together.

I'm not so sure. What it does is tell us what the limits of permissible dissent are. It lays down what it thinks are the parameters of debate. Radio Canada has always made the decision as to what is good for us.

When I was a little boy I used to listen to Hockey Night in Canada on Saturdays at six o'clock. They were all Toronto Maple Leaf games on the CBC assumption that all those outside Quebec should be Leaf fans. The CBC has always to my ear sounded like Ontario, especially Toronto.

When the Toronto CBC, which ruled English Canada, decided to broadcast and then televise the Hab's games, the team developed a new fan base who could see what a great team looked like.

This will startle CBC fans – they censor.

Three examples.

As mentioned earlier, when Gordon Campbell quit as BC Premier, I was a regular participant under contract in the political panel for CBC Morningside with Rick Cluff. We were all told that we would be asked to name the three best things and the three worst things Campbell had done. So like CBC – something nice for all.

I told them that I thought he was the worst Premier in history and that I could not think of a single redeeming feature about the man. I was told that if I wouldn't do as the CBC wished, I was told not to show up. Notwithstanding the fact that I was under contract I wasn't paid.

Minor censorship?

I, a well-known broadcaster on public affairs, wasn't welcome if my opinion differed from that of the "Mother Corp".

In 2012, after seven years on the panel I was suddenly fired. Why? Because I was too hard on Suzanne Anton, the BC Liberal representative and the government didn't like it. When I put this to the CBC, it wasn't denied.

The third revelation will come as a shock to CBC types – my late pal Stan Winfield simply could not believe me. But it's true – CBC censors its broadcasters.

A few years ago I subbed for Anna Marie Tremonti on **The Current** for a week, in Vancouver and Toronto. My first interview was with Cindy Sheehan, a mother who had lost her son in Iraq, and who was camped on George W. Bush's ranch in protest. In front of me were five or six questions which I took as being a helpful aide memoire.

I could not believe it when, the interview humming along nicely, I heard, in my ear, "Go to question two!" This happened during every interview over the next five shows, and each time I contented myself with a mental "fuck you". I could not believe it – CBC structures interviews and hosts ignore the questions on their little helpful sheet at some risk. *One can only assume from this that guests are advised on what subjects the broadcasters will cover.*

As I say, loyal CBC listeners tell me that they can't believe it – believe it!

I happen to support the CBC in principle and have so editorialized on more than one occasion. I think, however, by keeping outspoken people away from their employment is massive censorship that helps the Establishment in this country get away with murder.

Finis

There you have it – 25 years that I was lucky to live where I did and do what I did.

I have a very strong sense of gratitude for all who helped me and put up with me. Mostly I'm grateful for the super support I received from listeners, most of whom I knew their mood before I had even taken a call. I believe in that sort of telepathy as I felt all those many shows.

I'm especially grateful to Ted Smith who gave me a chance when I was down and out and supported me during trying times, to Ron Bremner (especially for his steadfastness during the Vander Zalm days), to Rod Gunn who stuck with me during some nasty legal dust-ups and to all the wonderful people I had the good luck to work with in all three stations for whom I broadcast.

In the words of Vera Lynn's great wartime chant, "Bless 'em all".